BAKING

FOOD52

BAKING

60 SENSATIONAL TREATS YOU CAN PULL OFF IN A SNAP

Editors of Food52

Photography by James Ransom

TEN SPEED PRESS
Berkeley

Contents

CUSTARDY CAKES & PUDDINGS

EVERYDAY CAKES

SPECIAL OCCASION CAKES

SAVORY BAKED GOODS

Foreword

One of us considers herself a baker; the other does not. Yet we both bake frequently at home. Amanda has had more formal training (the idea of rolling out pie dough or making a yeast bread doesn't give her the shakes), but Merrill also grew up enjoying homemade baked goods. So while only one of us could assemble a croquembouche without breaking a sweat, we both believe in a more uncommitted style of day-to-day baking.

When we talk about "uncommitted baking" (that was actually the first title for this book, which went over like rain at a beach party), we mean the kind of baking you can do on a weeknight, once the dinner dishes are cleared away and the kids are asleep—without having to stay up so late that you're bleary-eyed the next day. It's the kind of baking you can take on, like Amanda does, as a fun activity with her eight-year-old twins; each weekend, they make a simple cake to have around the house for packed lunches and after-dinner dessert during the week ahead.

We're talking about one-bowl cakes, cookies that don't require dipping or finishing, slumps, crisps, quick breads, galettes, puddings, and muffins. This is the sort of baking your grandmother did—unpretentious and comforting. Each recipe comes with tips and tricks learned from years of practice, in the voice of one home baker speaking to another. None of these recipes will keep you in the kitchen for hours just for the sake of it, and each produces consistently delicious results. We wanted to create a book that would be your right hand whenever a baked good beckoned.

The recipes come from our readers, contributors, and team members. Many are treasured family recipes that have never appeared on the site; others are from Food52 and have become legends in our office. Our former editor Marian Bull introduced us to her family's beloved schlumpf, an even more relaxed version of a crumble; with a name like schlumpf how could it not make it into this book? There are light-as-air berry scones from longtime Food52er mrslarkin, whose professional nickname is The Scone Lady. And we included Merrill's mother's recipe for cream cheese cookies, which have earned a bit of a cult following over the years among those addicted to their crisp, caramelized edges and chewy, slightly tangy centers.

All of these memorable recipes were expertly herded and curated by our editor Sarah Jampel. Sarah is like a whirling dervish, editing, styling, and coordinating—she'd complete a chapter or two before we finished our morning coffee. She left no stone unturned, and even pilfered many of her mom's own baking pans for this book's photo shoots. Under her careful direction, a baking book took shape that we hope will be an indispensable resource for bakers and nonbakers alike.

—Amanda Hesser & Merrill Stubbs

Introduction

The key to being a good baker is choosing good recipes. Yes, it's important to carefully follow the directions and to buy the right ingredients, but the real secret to successful baking is finding recipes that are guaranteed to turn out cookies, cakes, pies, and dinner rolls that not only taste much better than anything you could pick up from the store, but also make you smile involuntarily and maybe even bop up and down a little.

At Food52, we believe that no matter how busy you are, how much you hate messes, and how strongly you believe in your inability to follow a recipe, you don't need to outsource baking to the professionals. Anyone can have fresh biscuits in the morning and homemade brown sugar shortbread to snack on in the afternoon, and it needn't require huge amounts of time or energy. It's about finding reliable, no-fail recipes, baking them often, and, along the way, learning a handful of useful tips that will make you a better baker.

In this book, you'll find the kind of recipes that you know will provide delicious results without occupying your entire day, that you can make on a weeknight and enjoy for days after, and that are more fun than stressful and more satisfying than frustrating. These recipes come from old neighborhood cookbooks, from scribbled recipe cards stored in grandparents' kitchens, from bake sales of years past, and from friends whose desserts were the stars of every potluck. And since these recipes live in so many places, we use our website to collect and preserve the cookies and the cakes, the biscuits and the breads that have lived long, happy lives in kitchens just like yours.

In order to whittle down the huge assortment of outstanding recipes on our site to find the most beloved (and least fussy), we polled our staff and our trusted community members and, like always, they delivered. The sixty recipes we ended up with are all gems; each one had the Food52 editors speaking a little too loudly, trying to share stories of the first time we had tasted the Cardamom Currant Snickerdoodles (page 29) or made the Cheese Crispettes (page 134). This collection spans regions and time periods: "Cuppa Cuppa Sticka" Peach and Blueberry Cobbler (page 67)— named for the quantities of milk, sugar, and butter—from Gaffney, South Carolina; lemon custard unearthed in an old recipe box in an aunt's house in Virginia (page 79); Overnight Orange Refrigerator Rolls (page 19) from

Alabama; the chocolate cake Amanda ate for every birthday celebration growing up (page 96); mandelbrot studded with dark chocolate and dried cherries from North Dakota (page 34); and coconut-pecan bars that associate editor Sarah Jampel's grandma discovered in a cooking class on Long Island in the 1960s (page 42).

But despite the diversity of recipes in this book, they're all part of the same family. Turn to these easy-going standbys when it's Monday evening and you have little time or patience to fuss over buttercream, but also when you're in need of a dinner party dessert to surprise and impress guests. These recipes won't ask you to devote hours to baking, but they'll deliver the same satisfaction as if they had taken all day. Some, like the baked French toast (page 5), can be made ahead of time; others, like the Yogurt Biscuits (page 8), require no planning at all; and many, like the Brown Butter Cupcake Brownies (page 102), are perfect for baking on a rainy day and storing in the freezer for when you're in need of spontaneous chocolate.

Don't look here for yet another chocolate chip cookie recipe—but we're betting the Grape-Nut and Chocolate Chip Kitchen Sink Oatmeal Cookies (page 30) will become a new favorite. And while you might have eaten tres leches at a restaurant, we think that the coconut version on page 83 will be more interesting than anything you've tasted before (and best of all, you'll learn how simple it is to make this cake at home). Many of these recipes make use of a wide range of ingredients—like coconut oil, rye flour, black sesame seeds, and coconut milk—that add new dimensions of flavor and texture to baking yet are not difficult to find. Others—like the Honey Pecan Cake (page 92) or the Six-Ingredient Peanut Butter and Jelly Sandwich Cookies (page 33)—make use of pantry staples you already have on hand. And none of them will have you furrowing your brow over where to find acetate cake wrappers or how to fold puff pastry dough.

We hope this book empowers you to make your own whole wheat dinner rolls and to turn summer fruit into a jammy, flaky galette. When you slice into your homemade pizza dough for the first time, you'll find that the results are tastier and more satisfying than anything you could buy from the grocery store. Plus, you'll have the pleasure of knowing you made it yourself. Go ahead and dog-ear the pages. Splatter them with milk, sprinkle them with flour, and cover them with your own notes. Make a pile of cookies and feed them to your friends and family—just be prepared to share the recipes.

Baking Basics

Throughout the book, you'll find accompanying tips and tricks to make baking easier and more enjoyable (and to serve as a resource as you explore more recipes in the future). Here's a quick guide.

Breakfast Goods

Featherweight Blueberry Scones

MAKES 8 SCONES

2 ½ cups (315g) all-purpose flour

¼ cup (50g) sugar, plus more for sprinkling

1 tablespoon baking powder

¾ teaspoon kosher salt

6 tablespoons (85g) cold unsalted butter, cut into small pieces

¾ cup (about 115g) frozen blueberries (preferably wild Maine blueberries)

1 cup (240ml) heavy cream, plus more for mixing and brushing

1 egg

1½ teaspoons vanilla extract

Scones have a bad reputation for being either as crumbly as sand or as dense as paperweights, and good recipes are hard to come by. But when we received this recipe from Liz Larkin (aka, Food52er mrslarkin)—who is so revered for her scones that she's known as the "Scone Lady"—we knew it must be special. And it is. Make these scones with a light hand and a lot of cream, and they're sure to be tender, light, and loaded with berries.

To prevent frozen berries from leaving your scones with an odd greenish tint, you can rinse them in cold water several times until the water that drains off is noticeably lighter in color. Tossing the berries with the flour and the other dry ingredients before incorporating a wet mixture will also help seal them in a protective coating. To keep your scones attractive-looking and light in texture, be sure to fold the frozen berries into the batter gently—vigorous stirring will cause their color to bleed and the final product to be dense.

Serve these scones with clotted cream, crème fraîche, or jam if you wish. They are great the next day, warmed in the microwave for 15 to 20 seconds, and freeze well too: just reheat them in a 350°F (175°C) oven until warm.

---

1. Put the flour, sugar, baking powder, and salt in a food processor and pulse to combine. Add the butter and pulse about ten times. Don't process the heck out of it—some small pieces of butter should remain.

2. Transfer the flour mixture to a large bowl. If any really large lumps of butter remain, squish them with the back of a fork. Add the berries and gently toss to coat.

3. In a small bowl, combine the cream, egg, and vanilla and mix well. Pour into the flour mixture and use a fork or your hands to work the cream into the flour mixture as you gradually rotate the bowl; aim for a folding motion, not a stirring motion. When dough begins to come together, use a plastic bowl scraper, a sturdy plastic spatula, or your hands to gently work the dough into a ball. If there's still a lot of loose flour in the bottom of the bowl, drizzle in a bit more cream, about 1 teaspoon at a time, until the dough comes together.

CONTINUED

4. Transfer the dough to a floured work surface and gently pat it into a 6- to 7-inch (15 to 18cm) circle. With a pastry scraper or large chef's knife, cut the circle into 8 wedges. If you like, you can use a pie marker to score the top of the circle and then use those lines as a guide for cutting.

5. The next step is optional but recommended: Put the scones on a baking sheet lined with waxed paper and freeze until solid. (Once they're frozen, you can store them in a plastic freezer bag for several weeks.)

6. Preheat the oven to 425°F (220°C). If baking from frozen, preheat the oven to 400°F (205°C). Line a baking sheet with parchment paper.

7. Place the scones on the lined pan, about 1 inch (2.5cm) apart. Brush the tops with cream and then sprinkle with sugar.

8. Bake for 10 minutes, then rotate the pan and bake for 10 to 15 minutes longer, until a toothpick inserted into the center of a scone comes out clean. If baking from frozen, your scones will likely need an additional 5 minutes.

9. Let the scones rest for 5 minutes on the baking sheet before transferring to a wire rack to cool or serving warm.

For Something Different

Oatmeal Berry Scones (pictured on page 3) Substitute 1 cup (90g) of rolled oats (not quick oats) for 1 cup (125g) of the all-purpose flour and sprinkle a few oats on top of the scones before baking.

Lavender Blueberry Scones Add 1 tablespoon of crushed organic lavender (fresh or dried) when you add the berries to the flour. Sprinkle a few lavender buds on top of the scones before baking.

Ginger Lemon Scones Replace the blueberries with about ¼ cup (40g) chopped crystallized ginger and the zest of 1 lemon.

Whole Wheat Scones Substitute whole wheat for half of the all-purpose flour.

Savory Scones Omit the berries and vanilla, decrease the sugar to 2 tablespoons, and add in 1 tablespoon of your favorite herb (minced if fresh) to the flour mixture. Sprinkle flaky sea salt over the tops of the scones before baking.

Baked Cardamom French Toast with Syrupy Meyer Lemons

SERVES AT LEAST 10

French Toast

1 loaf (750g) white or whole wheat Pullman bread, slightly stale

Maple syrup, for drizzling between the bread layers

5 cups (1.2 L) milk or half-and-half

2 tablespoons cardamom pods (about 50), lightly crushed

6 tablespoons (90ml) sweetened condensed milk, plus more as needed

6 large eggs

1 teaspoon vanilla extract

1 teaspoon kosher salt

2 tablespoons raw sugar

1 tablespoon unsalted butter, cut into small pieces

Meyer Lemon Topping

1½ cups (300g) granulated sugar

1½ cups (355ml) water plus 2 teaspoons

3 Meyer lemons

2 teaspoons cornstarch

French toast may seem like a casual, low-maintenance breakfast until you understand the reality: there will be *stations*. You have to soak the bread, fry the bread, and keep the finished pieces warm. The good news is that you can avoid all that fussing by assembling the French toast the night before and baking it in the morning while you take a shower and make coffee. You'll still have enough time (and energy) to zest, juice, and slice some Meyer lemons for a sweet citrus syrup. After barely any early morning work, you'll end up with a dish that has a crunchy top and a custardy interior—and that's miraculously lighter and less oily than diner-style French toast.

---

1. To make the French toast, butter a 9 by 13-inch (23 by 33cm) baking pan. Slice the bread ½ inch (1.3cm) thick and arrange as many slices as you can fit in one layer in the prepared pan. Drizzle with maple syrup, then add another layer of bread. Repeat until all the bread has been used or the baking pan is full.

2. Combine the milk and cardamom pods in a medium saucepan. Cook over medium-high heat, just until almost simmering. Remove from the heat, cover, and let steep for 10 minutes.

3. Strain the milk into a large bowl through a fine-mesh sieve, then stir in the sweetened condensed milk. Taste and, if it isn't sweet enough, add more sweetened condensed milk by the tablespoon. Add the eggs, vanilla, and salt and whisk until smooth. Pour evenly over the bread. Cover and refrigerate overnight or for at least 6 hours.

4. The next day, or when you're ready to bake, preheat the oven to 350°F (175°C).

5. Sprinkle the raw sugar and the butter over the bread. Put the dish in a large roasting pan and add about 1 inch (2.5cm) of very hot tap water. Cover the roasting pan with aluminum foil, tenting it so it doesn't touch the surface, and make two slashes in the foil so that steam can escape.

CONTINUED

6. Bake for 45 minutes, then uncover and bake for 15 to 20 minutes longer, until the custard is set and the top layer of bread is crispy.

7. Meanwhile, make the Meyer lemon topping. In a small saucepan over medium heat, combine the granulated sugar with the 1½ cups (355ml) water and heat, stirring occasionally, until the sugar has completely dissolved. Add the grated zest and juice of one Meyer lemon and bring the mixture to a simmer; cook until reduced by a third, about 10 minutes.

8. Next, slice the two remaining lemons into thin disks, add them to the sugar mixture, and simmer for another 10 minutes. In a separate bowl, mix the cornstarch with the 2 teaspoons of cold water, whisking until it resembles heavy cream. Add this to the saucepan with the candied lemons and syrup, then bring the mixture to a simmer for another minute, until the syrup has slightly thickened. Rewarm the syrup gently before either pouring it over the finished French toast in the pan or drizzling over individual dishes.

9. Keep leftover French toast in the refrigerator for up to 3 days, reheating it gently in a warm oven.

For Something Different

Roasted Fig Topping Stem and halve 2 pounds (900g) of ripe figs. Put them on a baking pan in a single layer, cut side up. Combine ¼ cup (60g) unsalted butter, ¼ cup (60ml) maple syrup, and a generous pinch of salt in a small saucepan over medium heat and cook, stirring occasionally, until the butter is melted. Drizzle over the figs and bake, uncovered, in the oven with the French toast for about 20 minutes, until the figs are soft and juicy. Allow the French toast to cool for a few minutes in the dish, then serve it topped with the roasted figs and additional maple syrup.

How to Stale Fresh Bread in a Hurry

If you want to make baked French toast or bread pudding but only have fresh bread on hand, you don't have to wait a couple of days for that loaf to stale. Simply cut it into slices or cubes, depending on the recipe, and bake briefly in a 350°F (175°C) oven to wick off some of its moisture. After 15 to 20 minutes, the bread will be lightly brown, dry, and ready to use.

Yogurt Biscuits

MAKES 5 LARGE BISCUITS OR 10 SMALL BISCUITS

2 cups (250g) all-purpose flour

1 tablespoon baking powder

1 teaspoon salt

½ cup (120ml) plain yogurt

½ cup (120ml) milk (any type)

Milk or melted unsalted butter, for brushing (optional)

Coarse or flaky sea salt, for sprinkling

You can stop wondering whether you should have a responsible bowl of yogurt for breakfast or a plate of flaky biscuits instead. With this recipe you can have both—all at once (and easily, too). If you have flour, salt, yogurt, and you can stir, you're halfway there.

1. Preheat the oven to 375°F (190°C). Line a baking sheet with parchment paper.

2. Into a medium bowl, sift together the flour, baking powder, and salt.

3. In a separate bowl, stir the yogurt and milk together, then gradually add this to the flour mixture and mix gently until evenly incorporated; use a motion similar to cutting in butter (folding and smashing as opposed to stirring), and stop when the dough is still crumbly rather than making it into one homogenous ball.

4. Turn the dough out onto a floured surface and gently knead; to avoid overworking the dough, fold it over onto itself repeatedly and press down to work it together. As soon as the dough comes together in a unified mass, roll it out to form a flattened disk about 2 inches (5cm) high.

5. Using a round cutter, cut out biscuits and place them on the lined baking sheet. Gather any scraps and gently knead them together, working the dough as little as possible, then cut out more rounds. Gently brush their tops with a bit of milk or melted butter, then sprinkle with sea salt.

6. Bake for 10 to 15 minutes, until just barely golden brown (they will be paler if you did not brush them). Serve warm with plenty of butter.

For Something Different

Cheese Biscuits Dial the salt back to ½ teaspoon and add a scant ½ cup (about 55g) of shredded cheese and ¼ cup (25g) of thinly sliced green onions to the flour mixture.

Cinnamon-Sugar Biscuits Use just a pinch of salt and add 1 tablespoon of sugar to the flour mixture. Separately, mix together ¼ cup (50g) of sugar and 1 teaspoon of ground cinnamon. Instead of sprinkling the biscuits with coarse salt just before baking, top them with melted butter and the cinnamon sugar.

Cranberry, Oatmeal, and Flaxseed Muffins

MAKES 24 MUFFINS

5 cups (450g) rolled oats

2⅓ cups (280g) whole wheat flour

1½ cups (300g) light brown sugar

⅔ cup (75g) ground flaxseed or flaxseed meal

4 teaspoons baking soda

1 teaspoon baking powder

4 teaspoons ground cinnamon

½ teaspoon salt

2 eggs, lightly beaten

2 cups (475ml) buttermilk

1 cup (240ml) neutral oil, such as vegetable oil or mild coconut oil

¾ cup (175ml) water

2 cups (200g) fresh or frozen cranberries

These muffins, adapted from Brooklyn's Du Jour Bakery (Merrill's favorite), are the best of both worlds: the rolled oats and whole wheat flour make them a hearty, wholesome breakfast, while the baking powder and baking soda provide the airy lightness that's too often absent from healthier baked goods. Plenty of cinnamon plus a smattering of sweet-tart cranberries make the muffins seem sweeter than they actually are. Feel free to substitute any type of fresh, frozen, or even dried berry for the cranberries. And if you don't believe our testament to these muffins' greatness, ask Merrill's toddler Clara; this is the only breakfast that can entice her away from her usual toast and yogurt.

1. Preheat the oven to 350°F (175°C). Line two standard-sized muffin pans with paper liners.

2. In a large bowl, stir together the oats, flour, brown sugar, ground flaxseed, baking soda, baking powder, cinnamon, and salt. Add the eggs, buttermilk, oil, and water and mix until just combined. Fold in the cranberries. Spoon the batter into the lined muffins cups, filling each to the top.

3. Bake for 20 to 25 minutes, until a toothpick inserted into the center of a muffin comes out clean.

4. Let cool in the pans for 5 minutes, then transfer to a wire rack and let cool completely before serving.

How to Make Buttermilk at Home

To make a perfectly good substitute for buttermilk, simply measure out an amount of milk just shy of the amount of buttermilk called for. Then add a bit of white vinegar or lemon juice—about 1 tablespoon for every 1 cup (240ml) of buttermilk you need. Mix well, then let stand at room temperature for 5 to 10 minutes, until you see lumps when you stir the mixture around. If it doesn't curdle, add a bit more vinegar or lemon juice. Your makeshift buttermilk won't be as thick as the store-bought variety, but it will do the trick.

Whole Wheat Molasses Yogurt Bread with Figs and Walnuts

MAKES 1 LOAF; SERVES 12 TO 14

2 ½ cups (300g) white whole wheat flour, or a blend of 1 ¾ cups (210g) white whole wheat flour and ¾ cup (100g) rye flour

½ cup (80g) medium-or coarse-grind cornmeal

1 teaspoon kosher salt

1 teaspoon baking soda

1 ⅔ cups (395ml) whole-milk yogurt, or 1 ½ cups (355ml) whole milk plus 2 tablespoons white vinegar or apple cider vinegar

½ cup (120ml) molasses

1 cup (100g) toasted walnuts, chopped

¾ cup (105g) coarsely chopped dried figs

1 teaspoon unsalted butter

Finally, a quick bread recipe that passes all the tests of a great quick bread. First, it's quick: mix the wet ingredients, mix the dry ingredients, then combine them. Second, it's bread: it's less sweet than it is sturdy, hearty, and healthy, and it's suitable for spreading with butter, sprinkling with salt, and enjoying before noon. Third, it's hard to mess up and amendable to countless variations: learn the template, then substitute different types of flour, replace the molasses with honey, use milk instead of yogurt, and throw in any fruits and nuts you'd like. Store this recipe, adapted from Mark Bittman's *How to Cook Everything Vegetarian*, in your proverbial back pocket—it's one for the keeping.

---

1. Preheat the oven to 325°F (165°C). If using milk rather than yogurt, mix it with the vinegar.

2. In a large bowl, stir together the flour, cornmeal, salt, and baking soda.

3. Separately, whisk together the yogurt and molasses. Add to the flour mixture in two or three additions, stirring in round, sweeping motions and making sure to incorporate the flour at the bottom of the bowl; mix until just a few small pockets of flour remain. The dough may fizz subtly, like a science experiment, and it will be quite thick. Fold in the walnuts and figs.

4. Put the butter in either a standard loaf pan or a 7-inch (18cm) cast-iron skillet and put it in the oven until the butter melts. Tilt and swirl the pan to coat it evenly. Gently transfer the batter to the buttered pan without mixing it any further. It's okay if the top is a little lumpy—resist the urge to smooth it.

5. Bake until a toothpick inserted into the center comes out clean, about 50 minutes to 1 hour. Touch the top of the bread; it should give a bit and feel supple but resist your touch and not feel like there's goo beneath.

6. Very important: Let the bread cool completely before slicing it. Yes, we're serious. Wrap any leftovers tightly in foil and eat within 3 to 4 days.

Bestest Banana Bread

MAKES 1 LOAF; SERVES 12 TO 14

4 very ripe bananas, peeled

¼ cup (60g) unsalted butter, melted and cooled

1 egg, at room temperature

1 to 2 teaspoons vanilla extract

1 cup (200g) sugar

1½ cups (190g) all-purpose flour

1 teaspoon salt

1 teaspoon baking soda

1 teaspoon ground cinnamon

1 cup (240ml) plain yogurt

This banana bread is not just an easy solution to the pile of overripe bananas on your counter; it's so good that it's a reason to *let* those bananas freckle and slouch. It's a no-frills recipe that delivers on big banana flavor and is intuitive enough to learn by heart. If you'd like to elaborate, add a handful of chocolate chips, a tablespoon or two of peanut butter, or some chopped, toasted nuts. It's delicious warm, especially spread with butter or cream cheese and sprinkled with cinnamon, and it gets even better after a day or two.

1. Preheat the oven to 350°F (175°C). Butter a standard loaf pan.

2. Mash the bananas in a stand mixer fitted with a paddle attachment. You should have approximately 2 cups (475ml) of bananas.

3. Add the butter, egg, vanilla, and sugar and mix well.

4. In a small bowl, stir together the flour, salt, baking soda, and cinnamon. Fold into the banana mixture, and then gently fold in the yogurt.

5. Pour the batter into the prepared pan and bake for 50 minutes to 1 hour and 10 minutes, until the top is golden brown and springs back to the touch; a tester inserted into the middle of the loaf will come out with a few moist crumbs. (By the way, it's delicious a tad underbaked.)

6. Put the pan on a wire rack and let cool completely before turning the bread out and slicing. Wrap the leftovers tightly in foil and eat within 1 to 2 days.

How to Grind Fresh Spices

The easiest way to grind a large amount of fresh spices is to use an electric coffee or spice grinder. To grind cinnamon sticks, simply break the cinnamon sticks into manageable pieces and place them in an electric grinder, whirring until you have a fine powder. To grind cardamom, remove the seeds from the pods using a flat chef's knife: press down firmly on the pod (the same way you would smash a clove of garlic), then pry open the shell, pick out the seeds, and pulverize until you've achieved a fine powder. For smaller amounts, you can use a mortar and pestle.

Buttermilk Dutch Baby
with Caramelized Pears

SERVES 6 TO 8

Dutch Baby

2 tablespoons unsalted butter

2/3 cup (85g) all-purpose flour

3 tablespoons granulated sugar

Pinch of salt

1/4 teaspoon ground nutmeg

1/2 teaspoon ground cinnamon

1/3 cup (80ml) buttermilk

3 eggs

1/2 teaspoon vanilla extract

Topping

2 pears, peeled and thinly sliced

3 tablespoons brown sugar

Pinch of ground cinnamon

2 tablespoons unsalted butter

Confectioners' sugar, for dusting (optional)

A Dutch baby is a giant balloon of a pancake that's made in a cast-iron skillet in the oven, which means you don't have to stand over a hot stove flipping individual pancakes and praying they'll be fluffy. This recipe balances the tang of buttermilk with the sweetness of caramelized pears for a perfect morning treat. Feel free to replace the pears with other fruity toppings like cooked apples, macerated berries, or lemon curd. Or, for an even simpler (and more traditional) finish, put a pat of butter in the middle of the pancake, squeeze some lemon juice over the top, and sprinkle the whole thing with confectioners' sugar.

---

1. Preheat the oven to 350°F (175°C).

2. To make the Dutch baby, heat the butter in a 9- or 10-inch (23 or 25cm) cast-iron skillet over medium heat. Cook, swirling often, until the butter begins to brown, about 8 minutes.

3. Meanwhile, whisk the flour, granulated sugar, salt, nutmeg, and cinnamon together in a medium bowl. Make a well in the center, then add the buttermilk, eggs, and vanilla. Whisk until the batter is smooth, 1 to 2 minutes.

4. Swirl the skillet to coat it evenly with the butter, then pour in the batter. Bake for 25 to 30 minutes, until golden and puffed.

5. Meanwhile, make the topping. Toss the pear slices with the brown sugar and cinnamon until evenly coated. Heat the butter in a large skillet over medium-high heat. When the skillet is very hot, add the pears and turn the heat down to medium. Cook the pears, stirring every few minutes to keep the slices coated in syrup, until they are tender and caramelized, 10 to 15 minutes depending on their ripeness.

6. Place the pears on top of the Dutch baby and, if you wish, dust everything with confectioners' sugar.

Overnight Orange Refrigerator Rolls

MAKES 24 ROLLS

Dough

1 cup (240ml) water

¼ cup (60g) unsalted butter

¼ cup (50g) shortening, preferably butter-flavored

7 tablespoons (85g) granulated sugar

¾ teaspoon salt

2¼ teaspoons (1 package) active dry yeast

1 egg, slightly beaten

3 cups (375g) all-purpose flour, or as needed

Filling

8 tablespoons (100g) unsalted butter, at room temperature

½ cup (100g) granulated sugar

1½ teaspoons finely grated orange zest

Glaze

2 cups (250g) confectioners' sugar

¼ cup (60ml) freshly squeezed orange juice

While you may think that having fresh-from-the-oven yeast rolls before noon is out of your reach, it can be done. Just mix the dough in the evening, then roll, shape, and bake the buns in the morning. Altogether, the recipe requires only about 15 minutes of hands-on time, and baking the rolls in muffin tins with paper liners makes the process especially easy (and mess-free).

---

1. To make the dough, boil ½ cup (120ml) of the water in a small saucepan. Remove from the heat, add the butter and shortening, and stir until melted. Add the granulated sugar and salt and stir until combined. Let cool until lukewarm.

2. Heat the remaining ½ cup (120ml) water until it is between 105°F (40°C) and 115°F (45°C). Pour it into a large bowl, sprinkle the yeast over the top, and stir to dissolve the yeast. Stir in the sugar-butter-shortening mixture and the egg. Add the flour and mix thoroughly. If the dough is still sticky to the touch, add more flour, 1 tablespoon at a time, until the dough is smooth and no longer tacky. Cover and refrigerate for 8 to 10 hours, until doubled in size.

3. Meanwhile, make the filling. Stir together the butter, granulated sugar, and orange zest until completely combined. Set aside.

4. About 2 hours before serving, line two muffin pans with paper liners or butter three 8- or 9-inch (20 or 23cm) square baking pans.

5. Turn the dough out onto a floured work surface, divide it in half, and roll out each portion into an 8 by 12-inch (20 by 30cm) rectangle.

6. Spread half of the filling over each piece of dough. Roll up each rectangle to make an even, firm log, then slice each into 12 equal rounds. Put each round in a lined muffin cup, or arrange them in the prepared pans. Let rise for 1½ hours, until they've doubled in size and a finger indentation bounces back slowly but remains visible.

7. Preheat the oven to 375°F (190°C). Bake until lightly browned, about 15 minutes if using individual muffin cups and 20 minutes if using square baking pans.

8. Meanwhile, make the glaze. Stir together the confectioners' sugar and orange juice until smooth. Drizzle the glaze over the warm rolls.

Tomato and Cream Cheese Turnovers

MAKES 6 LARGE PASTRIES OR 12 SMALLER PASTRIES

6 ounces (170g) cream cheese, at room temperature

2 eggs

Salt and pepper

2 sheets all-butter puff pastry dough, defrosted

1 large tomato, sliced ¼ inch (6mm) thick

2 tablespoons sesame seeds

What's the quickest way to make any food feel fancy? With puff pastry, of course. To transform a classic bagel order—tomato and cream cheese on sesame—into something special, Food52 contributor Emily Vikre (aka, fiveandspice) defrosts puff pastry in the refrigerator overnight, rolls it out in the morning, and uses it to make flaky pockets filled with fresh tomatoes and cream cheese. Sprinkled with sesame seeds and baked until golden brown, the result is a glorious version of your favorite bagel.

1. Preheat the oven to 375°F (190°C).

2. Put the cream cheese, one of the eggs, and a couple pinches of salt and pepper in a large bowl. Using an electric mixer or stirring vigorously by hand, beat until smooth.

3. On a floured surface, roll one sheet of puff pastry out to a thickness of about ⅛ inch (3mm). Cut it into 6 rectangles.

4. For small pastries, spread one-twelfth of the cream cheese mixture on each rectangle, leaving a ¼-inch (6mm) margin around the edges. Distribute half of the tomato slices among the pastries, then fold each pastry square over to enclose the filling and firmly press the edges with a fork to seal. Repeat with the next sheet of puff pastry.

5. For large pastries, put one-sixth of the filling on each of the first 6 rectangles, leaving a ¼-inch (6mm) margin around the edges. Distribute all of the tomato slices among the pastries. Roll out the second sheet of puff pastry to the same size, cut it into 6 rectangles, and place one on top of each of the first 6 rectangles. Press the edges firmly with a fork to seal.

6. Transfer the pastries to two baking sheets. Whisk the remaining egg with a tiny splash of water to make an egg wash, then brush it over the pastries. Sprinkle with the sesame seeds.

7. Bake for about 25 minutes, until golden brown and puffed.

8. Transfer to a wire rack and let cool slightly. Enjoy them right away—these pastries are definitely best eaten fresh.

Cookies & Bars

Cream Cheese Cookies

MAKES ABOUT 24 COOKIES

½ cup (110g) unsalted butter (preferably a less expensive one with a high water content and a low fat content, like Land O'Lakes), at room temperature

3 ounces (85g) cream cheese, at room temperature

1 cup (200g) sugar

1 cup (125g) all-purpose flour

½ teaspoon salt

Merrill's mother got the recipe for these cookies at a Tupperware party in the 1970s, but don't let that make you a skeptic: it's simply an indication of just how perfect these cookies are to keep tucked away for surprise guests or spur-of-the-moment gifts. Their chewy centers have a texture like a coconut macaroon, while the edges are buttery, burnished, and crumbly. But what truly makes these cookies special—and addictive—is the cream cheese, which provides an irresistible tang you'll recognize from cheesecakes and the frosting of your favorite carrot cake.

1. Preheat the oven to 350°F (175°C). Line two baking sheets with parchment paper.

2. Put the butter, cream cheese, and sugar in a large bowl. Using a handheld electric mixer or a stand mixer fitted with a paddle attachment, beat until light and fluffy, 3 to 5 minutes. Add the flour and salt and mix just until incorporated. Scrape down the bowl and give the batter a quick stir with a spoon to make sure everything is evenly mixed.

3. Drop the batter by the heaping tablespoon onto the lined baking sheets, spacing each one about 1½ inches (4cm) apart to allow for spreading.

4. Bake for about 12 to 14 minutes, until the edges are golden brown. Don't overbake, or the cookies won't be chewy.

5. Let cool slightly on the baking sheet, then transfer to a wire rack to cool completely. Store in an airtight container for up to 5 days.

How to Accurately Measure Flour

Not all cups of flour are created equal, which is why precise bakers use a scale, the only way to guarantee that there are 125 grams of all-purpose flour for every cup. The next best way to measure flour is to spoon and sweep: Aerate the flour by stirring it with a whisk, then spoon it into a measuring cup, overfilling it. Sweep the excess flour away with the straight edge of a knife. This results in a cup of flour that weighs close to 125 grams. In comparison, when you plunge the cup into the flour bin, you may end up with as much as 170 grams, resulting in baked goods that are too dense.

Italian Cornmeal Cookies

MAKES ABOUT 32 COOKIES

1 cup (125g) all-purpose flour

¼ cup (30g) fine cornmeal

½ cup (100g) sugar

⅔ cup (150g) cold unsalted butter, cut into small pieces

2 egg yolks

Zest of 1 lemon, finely grated

The recipe for these delicate golden cookies with a good crunch comes from the Piedmont region in northern Italy, where they are known as *biscotti di meliga*. Serve them as an after-dinner treat accompanied by creamy *zabaglione* (egg custard) and a glass of Italian wine like Moscato or Dolcetto, or enjoy them with espresso or tea in the afternoon.

If you can't find fine cornmeal, measure out a little over ¼ cup of regular cornmeal and blitz it in the food processor for 10 to 20 seconds, until it's noticeably powdery and a bit of cornmeal dust has started to rise.

---

1. Preheat the oven to 350°F (175°C).

2. In a large bowl, stir together the flour, cornmeal, and sugar and add the butter. Mix with an electric mixer or work the ingredients together with your hands until the texture is similar to breadcrumbs. Add the egg yolks and zest and mix or stir to form a smooth ball of dough. Wrap the ball of dough in plastic wrap and refrigerate for at least 30 minutes or up to 12 hours.

3. Roll out the dough on a well-floured surface to a thickness of just under ½ inch (1.3cm). Cut out rounds with a cookie cutter about 2 inches (5cm) in diameter. Transfer to a baking sheet, or two baking sheets if need be, lined with parchment paper or Silpat. The cookies can be closely spaced, as they don't spread much during baking. Transfer the baking sheet to the freezer and freeze for at least 30 minutes.

4. Bake for 13 to 15 minutes, until golden and slightly puffy.

5. Let the cookies cool completely on the baking sheet before serving. Store leftovers in an airtight container for 3 to 4 days.

How to Deal with Sticky Cookie Dough

If your stubborn dough insists on sticking, the solution is to sandwich it between two pieces of lightly floured parchment paper and roll from there. After rolling out the dough, remove the top sheet of parchment, cut out shapes with cookie cutters, and then gently tear away the excess dough. Slide the parchment paper onto the baking sheet, put the pan in the freezer for 10 to 15 minutes for the cookies to firm up and keep their shape, and then pop them into the oven.

Cardamom Currant Snickerdoodles

MAKES ABOUT 24 COOKIES

3 cups (375g) all-purpose flour

1 cup plus 3 tablespoons (235g) granulated sugar

½ cup (110g) packed brown sugar

2 teaspoons cream of tartar

1 teaspoon baking soda

½ teaspoon salt

2 teaspoons ground cardamom

1 cup (225g) unsalted butter, melted and cooled

3 eggs, lightly beaten

1 teaspoon vanilla extract

½ cup (75g) dried currants

Executive editor Kristen Miglore wouldn't rest until she secured a spot for these Food52 favorites in this book. If their ideal texture—soft, chewy, sandy, and crispy all at once—isn't enough to earn them a permanent place in your cookie jar, their flavor surely is. By replacing the usual cinnamon with the livelier cardamom, the classic snickerdoodle gets a whole new life. To optimize flavor, it's best if the cardamom is freshly ground (see page 15) or at least recently purchased. Keep these on hand for afternoon snacking or put them on a pretty plate at your holiday party; just be careful leaving a batch unattended—if you walk away, they'll be gone when you return.

---

1. Preheat the oven to 425°F (220°C).

2. In a medium bowl, stir together the flour, 1 cup (200g) of the granulated sugar, brown sugar, cream of tartar, baking soda, salt, and 1 teaspoon of the cardamom to combine.

3. In a separate bowl, whisk together the melted butter and eggs, then stir in the vanilla. Pour into the flour mixture, add the currants, and stir just until everything comes together to form a dough. Refrigerate for 10 minutes.

4. In a small bowl, stir together the remaining 3 tablespoons (35g) granulated sugar and 1 teaspoon cardamom. Roll the chilled dough into 1½-inch (4cm) balls, then roll each ball in the sugar mixture. Place the balls on baking sheets, spacing them about 2 inches (5cm) apart to allow for spreading.

5. Bake for 8 to 9 minutes, until golden and cracked on top but still a bit doughy in the middle.

6. Immediately transfer to a wire rack and let cool slightly. (Or eat them nice and warm off of the cooling rack with a cup of coffee or a glass of milk. No one will know some are missing!) Store in airtight container for 3 to 4 days.

Grape-Nut and Chocolate Chip Kitchen Sink Oatmeal Cookies

MAKES 24 TO 48 COOKIES, DEPENDING ON THE SIZE

1 cup (225g) unsalted butter

1 cup (200g) granulated sugar

½ cup (110g) packed brown sugar

2 eggs

2 teaspoons vanilla extract

3 cups plus 2 tablespoons (285g) rolled oats

1 cup (125g) all-purpose flour

½ cup (60g) whole wheat flour

½ cup (50g) wheat germ

1 teaspoon baking soda

1 teaspoon salt

1½ teaspoons ground cinnamon

1 cup (145g) raisins

1 cup (about 110g) toasted nuts, preferably pecans or walnuts, chopped

1 cup (175g) chocolate chips

1 cup (115g) Grape-Nuts cereal

½ cup (40g) unsweetened shredded dried coconut

Rarely will an oatmeal cookie have you jumping up and down, and rarely will oatmeal cookie dough have you sneaking spoonfuls before the baking sheet is in the oven. These cookies, however, will change all that. This recipe capitalizes on baking staples you're likely to have in your pantry—wheat germ, shredded coconut, raisins, and chocolate—to bring new life and flavor to an old standard. The real game changer, however, is Grape-Nuts cereal, a not-so-secret ingredient that adds crunch and a slight nuttiness. We recommend rolling the dough into balls and saving some in the freezer so that you'll always be just 15 minutes away from a warm, chewy cookie.

1. Preheat the oven to 350°F (175°C) and line two baking sheets with parchment paper.

2. Using a handheld electric mixer or a stand mixer fitted with the paddle attachment, beat the butter and both sugars until very pale and fluffy, about 3 to 5 minutes. Add the eggs and vanilla and mix well. In another bowl, mix together the rolled oats, flours, wheat germ, baking soda, salt, cinnamon, raisins, nuts, chocolate chips, cereal, and coconut. Add this dry mixture to the butter and egg mixture and stir until combined.

3. For smaller cookies, drop the dough with a tablespoon or a tablespoon-sized cookie scoop, allowing 2 inches (5cm) between each. For larger cookies, use an ice cream scoop or a ¼-cup (60ml) measure to portion the dough and allow for 3 inches (7.5cm) between each one.

4. Bake for 10 to 15 minutes, depending on the size of the cookies, until firm and golden brown at the edges. Cool on the baking sheet for 5 minutes and then transfer to a wire rack to cool completely. Store in an airtight container for up to 1 week.

Six-Ingredient Peanut Butter and Jelly Sandwich Cookies

MAKES 12 TO 14 SANDWICH COOKIES

1 cup (250g) peanut butter, plus more for filling the sandwich cookies

1 cup (200g) brown sugar

1 egg

1 teaspoon baking soda

1 teaspoon vanilla extract

Granulated sugar, for shaping cookies

About ¼ cup (60ml) jelly or jam, for filling the sandwich cookies

Flourless peanut butter cookies serve as the "bread" in this reimagined PB&J. Made with only six ingredients, they're soft and chewy with just the right amount of crispiness at the edges. You can use either smooth or chunky peanut butter depending on your preference (or what's in your pantry). Once the cookies cool a bit, all that's left to do is make them into sandwiches with a smear of peanut butter and a dollop of your favorite jam and enjoy them with a tall glass of cold milk.

---

1. Preheat the oven to 350°F (175°C). Line two large baking sheets with parchment paper.

2. Combine the peanut butter, brown sugar, egg, baking soda, and vanilla in a large bowl and stir well. Scoop out teaspoonfuls of the dough and put them on the lined baking sheets, spacing them 2 inches (5cm) apart to allow for spreading. Using a fork dipped in granulated sugar, gently press the cookies down. Rotate the fork and press again to make the classic peanut butter cookie crosshatch pattern. The dough is quite sticky, so keep sugaring the fork to prevent sticking.

3. Bake for 10 to 12 minutes, until the cookies are soft with light-colored tops but the edges are set and beginning to brown.

4. Let cool for a couple of minutes, then transfer to a wire rack and let cool completely.

5. Turn half of the cookies over and spread the flat side of each with a thin layer of peanut butter, then a teaspoonful of jam, spreading it almost to the edges of the cookies. Top with the remaining cookies. (For longer storage, keep the cookies in an airtight container for up to 3 to 4 days, then spread them with peanut butter and jelly right before serving.)

Dark Chocolate and Cherry Mandelbrot

MAKES 20 TO 24 COOKIES

5 ounces (140g) almond paste, chopped into small pieces

Confectioners' sugar, for coating the almond paste

3 cups (375g) all-purpose flour

1 teaspoon baking powder

¾ teaspoon kosher salt

1 cup (240ml) vegetable oil

1 cup plus 2 tablespoons (225g) granulated sugar

3 eggs

2 teaspoons vanilla extract

½ teaspoon almond extract

½ cup (85g) dark chocolate chips

½ cup (65g) dried sweet or sour cherries

Sea salt

2 to 4 tablespoons sliced almonds (optional)

If you're not familiar with mandelbrot (Yiddish for "almond bread"), they're like a friendlier, more forgiving version of biscotti: you don't need to pull out a hefty electric mixer or wrangle a super sticky dough to make them, but you do use the same technique of baking the cookies in a big log, then slicing the log and sending the cookies back into the oven to firm up. This less traditional take on mandelbrot uses almond paste to add pockets of softness and sweetness to an otherwise firm cookie. Because they have a long shelf life, they are perfect for sending in the mail as a gift.

———————————————————————

1. In a small bowl, toss the chopped almond paste with a bit of confectioners' sugar to prevent the pieces from sticking together. In a medium bowl, whisk together the flour, baking powder, and salt.

2. In a large bowl, whisk together the oil and 1 cup (200g) of granulated sugar. Whisk in the eggs one at a time, then the vanilla and almond extracts. While mixing with a wooden spoon, add the flour mixture. Add the almond paste pieces, chocolate chips, and cherries and stir to combine. Cover the dough with plastic wrap and refrigerate for at least an hour, and up to a day.

3. When you're ready to bake, preheat the oven to 350°F (175°C). Line a baking sheet with parchment paper. Divide the dough into two portions and orient them lengthwise on the lined baking sheet. Mold each into a long rectangle about 3 inches (7.5cm) wide, making sure to leave about 2 inches (5cm) of space between the logs. If the dough is sticky, lightly oil your hands.

4. Sprinkle the tops with the remaining 2 tablespoons of sugar, a few pinches of sea salt, and the sliced almonds. You may need to gently press the almonds into the dough for them to stick.

5. Bake for 25 to 30 minutes, until the center is set and the dough has lost some of its paleness. Remove from the oven and turn the oven temperature down to 250°F (120°C). Let the dough logs cool slightly, about 10 minutes, then use a serrated knife to slice them crosswise into pieces 1 inch (2.5cm) thick. Turn the slices on their sides, then bake for 20 minutes, or until they reach the desired crispness. Let cool for 2 to 5 minutes on the baking sheets, then transfer the mandelbrot to a wire rack to cool completely. Store the cookies in an airtight container for up to several weeks.

Brown Sugar Shortbread

MAKES 16 TO 32 PIECES

½ cup (110g) salted butter, at room temperature

¼ cup (50g) light brown sugar

1⅓ cups (160g) all-purpose flour

Merrill, who adapted this recipe from her grandmother, calls it "the easiest, most foolproof recipe in the world." If you have three basic ingredients, a wooden spoon, a baking pan, and a working oven, you can make it. The dough is incredibly simple, which means you can scale it up for parties and gift-giving. The brown sugar in the recipe lends a subtle caramel flavor, but if you only have white sugar on hand, it's fine to use that in its place.

Once you've mastered this recipe, try baking the shortbread for 15 to 20 minutes, until it's just the lightest shade of gold, letting it cool slightly, and then spreading your favorite fruit preserves over the top. Then bake for 10 to 15 minutes longer, until the jam is set. Ta-da! You've just made fruit bars.

1. Using an electric mixer or creaming vigorously with a wooden spoon, beat the butter and brown sugar until fluffy and pale. Add the flour and stir just until incorporated.

2. Transfer the dough to an 8-inch (20cm) cake pan (square or round) and press it into an even layer with your fingers. Prick the dough evenly across the surface with a fork. If you're using a square pan, score the dough into 6 rows and 4 columns (for 24 cookies) or into 8 rows by 4 columns (for 32 cookies) using a very sharp knife. If you're using a circular pan, score the dough into 16 or 24 triangles.

3. Cover with plastic wrap and refrigerate for at least 20 minutes before baking.

4. Preheat the oven to 325°F (165°C).

5. Bake for about 25 to 30 minutes, until the dough is a very light golden brown and the surface looks dry; watch carefully so it doesn't get too dark. (The shortbread will get darker as it cools in the pan, so you'll want to pull it out just before it has reached the desired color.)

6. Remove from the oven and immediately cut it using the scored lines as guides. Let cool in the pan before separating the pieces. The shortbread will keep in an airtight container for several days.

Balsamic Macaroons with Chocolate Chips

MAKES ABOUT 24 MACAROONS

3 egg whites

1 tablespoon balsamic glaze

2 teaspoons sugar

Large pinch of sea salt

2½ cups plus 2 tablespoons (210g) sweetened dried coconut flakes

½ cup (110g) mini semisweet chocolate chips

This recipe is an example of a science experiment gone terribly right. The combination of coconut, chocolate, and balsamic vinegar may seem strange, but one taste of these sweet, salty, and nutty cookies will change your mind.

The recipe calls for balsamic glaze, which you can either purchase or make yourself: just cook 1 cup (240ml) of balsamic vinegar in a saucepan over medium-low heat until it has reduced by half, about 20 minutes (you'll know it's finished when it coats the back of a metal spoon). Store extra balsamic glaze in a glass jar in the refrigerator for several weeks.

---

1. Preheat the oven to 350°F (175°C). Line a baking sheet with parchment paper.

2. In a large bowl, whisk together the egg whites, balsamic glaze, sugar, and salt until frothy. Fold in the coconut and chocolate chips.

3. Drop dollops of the mixture onto the lined baking sheet, using about 1½ tablespoons per macaroon. If they don't come off the spoon easily, wet your hands and gently form the dollops into small mounds. It's best to do this step near the kitchen sink so you can keep rewetting your hands.

4. Bake for 10 minutes, until dark golden brown.

5. Set the baking sheet on a wire rack and let the macaroons cool on the sheet for 5 minutes. Then transfer them to the rack and let cool completely.

How to Package Cookies for the Mail

Choose sturdy, somewhat hard or chewy cookies to send as gifts in the mail—like the mandelbrot (page 34), the Grape-Nut and Chocolate Chip Kitchen Sink Oatmeal Cookies (page 30), or the Brown Sugar Shortbread (page 37). Before packing the cookies, make sure they're completely cool. Put round, sturdy cookies that won't break in cellophane bags, and pack more delicate cookies in reusable containers or cookie tins, separating the layers with waxed paper. Be sure to fill empty areas of the shipping box with bubble wrap or newspaper. After that, all you need to do is call up your lucky recipients and remind them to check the mail.

Hippie Crispy Treats

MAKES 16 MEDIUM BARS

Bars

½ cup (120ml) maple syrup

½ cup (120ml) brown
rice syrup

½ cup (130g) almond butter

3⅓ ounces (95g) bittersweet
chocolate (70% cacao), chopped

2 tablespoons coconut oil

¼ teaspoon fine sea salt

4 cups (110g) crisp rice cereal

Topping

3⅓ ounces (95g) bittersweet
chocolate (70% cacao), chopped

2 tablespoons coconut oil

¼ cup (25g) toasted
sliced almonds

¼ teaspoon flaky sea salt

Here's what happens when your favorite childhood dessert grows up, goes to college, and joins a commune. These bars have the gooey nostalgia of Rice Krispies Treats, but the marshmallows are swapped out for a more sophisticated mixture of chocolate and almond butter. Add dried fruit, shredded coconut, or chopped nuts for a variation, and if you don't have rice and maple syrups, you can substitute corn syrup or golden syrup. This version has a top layer of chocolate ganache sprinkled with almonds and flaky salt, but if you love chocolate, double the ganache and shower the top with cacao nibs.

1. Line an 8-inch (20cm) square baking pan with parchment paper, allowing it to drape over the edges.

2. To make the bars, combine the maple and rice syrups in a large pan over medium-high heat. Bring to a boil and cook, stirring frequently, for 1 minute. Remove from the heat, add the almond butter, chocolate, coconut oil, and salt, and stir until the mixture is smooth and the chocolate is melted. Fold in the cereal.

3. Transfer the mixture to the lined pan and pack it firmly and evenly using a spatula or your fingers (you may want to dampen your fingers to prevent sticking).

4. To make the topping, combine the chocolate and oil in a small saucepan and cook over very low heat, stirring constantly, just until the chocolate has melted, then cool for 5 minutes.

5. To assemble the treats, pour the topping evenly over the rice mixture and smooth the top with a rubber spatula. Sprinkle the almonds and salt over the top.

6. Let set at cool room temperature for about 2 hours, or in the refrigerator for about 1 hour, until firm. Use the edges of the parchment paper to lift the bars out of the pan and cut into 16 squares.

7. These treats are at their very best the day they're made. They'll keep at room temperature for several days, though the cereal will soften slightly.

Double-Layer Coconut Pecan Bars

MAKES 36 SMALL BARS

Shortbread

½ cup (110g) unsalted butter, at room temperature

½ cup (100g) brown sugar

1 cup (125g) all-purpose flour

Topping

2 eggs

1 cup (200g) brown sugar

½ cup (40g) unsweetened shredded dried coconut

2 tablespoons all-purpose flour

1 teaspoon vanilla extract

1 cup (115g) pecans, chopped

½ teaspoon salt

These two-layers bars come from associate editor Sarah Jampel's grandmother, who learned about the recipe in a cooking class on Long Island in the 1960s. For fifty years, she's been cutting the bars into tiny squares and placing each one into a dainty white doily to serve to visitors, but we don't think anyone will complain if you slice them into much larger pieces. With their nutty top layer and flaky shortbread bottom, these bars emulate the rich caramel taste of a traditional pecan pie, yet they're much simpler to make. Feel free to substitute another type of nut, such as walnuts or cashews.

1. Preheat the oven to 375°F (190°C). Butter an 8-inch (20cm) square baking pan.

2. To make the shortbread, use an electric mixer or a wooden spoon to cream the butter and sugar together until pale and fluffy.

3. Stir in the flour, beating until just combined. Transfer the mixture to the prepared pan and press it evenly into the pan.

4. Bake for 20 minutes, until the shortbread is golden brown.

5. Meanwhile, prepare the topping. In a medium bowl, vigorously mix the eggs and sugar until well combined. Toss the coconut with the flour, then add it to the egg mixture, along with the vanilla, pecans, and salt.

6. Spread the topping over the shortbread and bake for 20 minutes longer, until the filling is browned on top and slightly puffed. Let cool completely before cutting into squares. Store in an airtight container in the refrigerator for 4 to 5 days.

How to Keep Brown Sugar Soft

To prevent brown sugar from hardening, open the bag and transfer the sugar to an airtight container. Put a marshmallow in the container to provide enough moisture to keep your sugar scoopable. And if you do find yourself with a solid lump of brown sugar, transfer it to a microwave-safe bowl, cover it with a damp paper towel, and microwave for 20- or 30-second intervals until it's soft.

Oatmeal Streusel Bars with Rhubarb Filling

MAKES 18 LARGE BARS

Filling

3 cups (375g) rhubarb cut into 1-inch (2.5cm) pieces

½ cup (100g) granulated sugar

2 heaping tablespoons cornstarch

¼ cup (60ml) cold water

1 tablespoon vanilla extract

Crust and Topping

1½ cups (135g) rolled oats

1½ cups (190g) all-purpose flour

1 cup (200g) light brown sugar

½ cup (50g) walnuts, finely chopped

½ teaspoon baking soda

½ teaspoon sea salt

1 cup (225g) unsalted butter, at room temperature

This recipe is like a chain letter. It comes from Food52 contributor Emily Vikre (aka, fiveandspice), who got it from her friend Kaitlin, who got it from someone named Rhea (the original name is Rhea's Rhubarb Bars). These crumb bars are hearty and wholesome thanks to the oats and walnuts, and they're sure to become a mainstay at potlucks and bake sales during rhubarb season. But when rhubarb is out of season, you can replace it with apricots, peaches, cranberries, or any other kind of berry. Use less cornstarch with peaches, cranberries, and other berries (they have enough natural pectin to thicken the filling), and use less sugar with sweet, ripe summer fruits. Feel free to use pecans or almonds in place of the walnuts.

1. To make the filling, combine the rhubarb and granulated sugar in a heavy saucepan. Cook over medium heat, stirring occasionally, until the rhubarb has broken down and is soupy, about 10 minutes.

2. Stir the cornstarch into the water to make a slurry, then stir that into the rhubarb and sugar mixture. Bring the mixture to a boil and cook, stirring occasionally, just until thick, 1 to 2 minutes. Remove from the heat and stir in the vanilla.

3. Preheat the oven to 350°F (175°C) and butter a 9 by 13-inch (23 by 33cm) baking pan.

4. To make the crust and topping, put the oats, flour, brown sugar, walnuts, baking soda, and salt in a medium bowl and stir to combine. Add the butter and use your fingers to work it in until the mixture is crumbly.

5. To assemble and bake the bars, transfer half of the mixture to the prepared pan and press it evenly across the bottom. Pour in the filling and spread it in an even layer. Sprinkle clumps of the remaining oat mixture over the filling.

6. Bake for 30 to 35 minutes, until bubbling and golden brown.

7. Let cool completely before cutting. For 2 by 3-inch (5 by 7.5cm) bars, cut into thirds lengthwise and sixths crosswise. The bars will keep for a couple of days, but cover them only loosely so they don't get too soggy.

Magic Espresso Brownies

MAKES 24 LARGE BROWNIES, OR 36 SMALLER BROWNIES

Brownies

3 cups (600g) lightly packed dark brown sugar

1 cup (225g) unsalted butter, at room temperature

8 extra-large eggs

1 tablespoon vanilla extract

⅛ teaspoon fine sea salt

1½ cups (190g) all-purpose flour

⅔ cup (30g) Dutch-processed cocoa powder

2 tablespoons instant espresso powder

2 cups (about 220g) toasted nuts, such as a mixture of pecans, walnuts, and hazelnuts, chopped

2 cups (340g) semisweet chocolate chips

Frosting

1¼ cups (250g) superfine sugar

2 tablespoons instant espresso powder

¼ cup (60ml) Cognac

¼ cup (60ml) whole milk

6 tablespoons (85g) unsalted butter

1 cup (170g) semisweet chocolate chips

It can take years to perfect your go-to brownie recipe for bake sales, late-night snacks, dinners with friends, and 4 p.m. chocolate cravings. Luckily, Food52er June Jacobs (aka, ChefJune) has done the work for us. This is the thirty-fifth iteration of her favorite basic brownie recipe, so there's no question it's good. What's "magic" about these brownies (there's nothing illegal about them) is how they're chewy, cakey, and fudgy all at the same time.

---

1. Preheat the oven to 350°F (175°C). Butter a 13 by 18-inch (33 by 45cm) half sheet pan.

2. First, make the brownies. Using an electric mixer on medium-low speed, mix the brown sugar and butter in a large bowl until well blended but not too fluffy. Add the eggs one at a time, mixing well after each addition and scraping down the sides of the bowl occasionally. Mix in the vanilla and salt.

3. In a medium bowl, stir together the flour, cocoa powder, espresso powder, and nuts. Pour into the sugar mixture and mix on low speed.

4. Pour the batter into the prepared pan and add the chocolate chips.

5. Bake for 23½ minutes (assuming your oven is calibrated properly). The batter will still be soft in the middle of the pan. Let the brownies cool completely before frosting.

6. To make the frosting, combine the superfine sugar, espresso powder, Cognac, milk, and butter in a heavy saucepan over medium heat. Cook, stirring constantly, until the mixture comes to a boil, then for 1 additional minute. Remove from the heat, add the chocolate chips, and stir until smooth.

7. Pour the frosting evenly over the cooled brownies. When the frosting has set, cut the brownies into squares of the desired size. Store the brownies in the refrigerator, separating the layers with parchment paper, for up to 3 days.

Fruit Desserts

Blueberry Schlumpf

MAKES ONE 8-INCH (20CM) SQUARE PAN; SERVES 8 TO 12

1 cup plus 2 tablespoons
(140g) all-purpose flour

2 tablespoons granulated
sugar

4 cups (about 600g) fresh
blueberries, preferably wild

½ cup (100g) brown sugar

½ cup (110g) salted butter,
at room temperature but not
yet soft, cut into small pieces

This dessert, bubbly and sweet and topped with a crust that's more cookie than cobbler, has become a cult favorite at Food52, and we have former editor Marian Bull's distant cousin Hasso Ewing's mother to thank. She makes it every summer up in Sorrento, Maine, using wild blueberries, but this recipe also works well with stone fruits and other berries. Whatever way you make it, be sure to have some good vanilla ice cream on hand to serve alongside. We recommend baking a double batch in a 9 by 13-inch (23 by 33cm) baking dish so you'll have leftovers for breakfast the next morning.

1. Preheat the oven to 375°F (190°C).

2. Sprinkle the 2 tablespoons (15g) of flour and the granulated sugar over the blueberries and stir gently until evenly coated. Transfer to an 8-inch (20cm) square baking pan.

3. Put the brown sugar, butter, and remaining 1 cup (125g) of flour in a medium bowl and stir with a fork or mix with your fingers just until the ingredients come together and form lumps. Sprinkle evenly over the blueberries.

4. Bake for 30 to 35 minutes, until the top is golden, caramel brown and beginning to sink and melt into the bubbling filling below. Serve hot, and enjoy the leftovers either cold or gently reheated in the oven or microwave.

How to Make Brown Sugar at Home

If you're halfway through a recipe that calls for brown sugar and you discover you don't have any, don't panic—you can make your own. Combine sugar and molasses in a food processor and process for a minute or two, pausing to scrape down the sides as necessary, until the molasses is evenly distributed. For light brown sugar, use 1 to 1½ tablespoons of molasses for every 1 cup (200g) of sugar; for darker brown sugar, use up to 4 tablespoons of molasses for every 1 cup (200g) of sugar.

Nectarine Slump

SERVES 10

About 1½ pounds (680g)
ripe, sweet nectarines, pitted
and quartered

1 cup (200g) sugar, plus more
for sprinkling

½ cup (110g) salted butter,
at room temperature

2 eggs

1⅓ cups (315ml) mascarpone

⅛ teaspoon almond or vanilla
extract

¼ cup (30g) all-purpose flour

A slump is the most easygoing member of the family of fruit-and-dough desserts, which also includes buckles, brown betties, crumbles, and grunts. Thanks to the indulgent addition of mascarpone, this slump's dough is extra fluffy. It's barely held together with flour, making it more like a custardy comforter laid atop the fruit than a traditional dough topping. The slump will taste best when made with ripe, sweet, fragrant stone fruit, and try it with whatever variety looks most appealing: peaches, apricots, or even plums. Enjoy this dessert outside on a summer evening and you'll find yourself slumping into relaxation.

1. Preheat the oven to 375°F (190°C). Generously butter a large, shallow baking dish measuring about 9 by 13 inches (23 by 33cm).

2. Arrange the nectarines in the baking dish; they should cover the bottom of the pan but not be jammed in too snugly. Sprinkle lightly with about 1 teaspoon of sugar.

3. Using a stand mixer fitted with a paddle attachment or a handheld electric mixer, beat the sugar and butter until fluffy and pale. Beat in the eggs, then the mascarpone and almond extract. Fold in the flour by hand, using a spatula. Spoon the mixture over the nectarines and spread it evenly until almost touching the edges of the pan.

4. Bake for 30 to 40 minutes, until the sides rise and the center is just set. Let cool before serving.

How to Pit Stone Fruits

To more easily pit stone fruit, stick a sharp knife into the top of the fruit, deep enough to feel the pit, and run the knife along the seam that goes from top to bottom to create two equal halves. Twist the halves in opposite directions, as you would an avocado or an Oreo. Use your thumb or a paring knife to pop the pit out of the flesh. For cherries, all you need is an empty bottle with a narrow mouth, such as a beer bottle or glass soda bottle, and a chopstick. Rest a cherry on the lip of the bottle and hold it gently. Press the chopstick through the cherry, pushing the pit out the other side and into the bottle below.

Apple Brown Betty with Gingersnap Crumbs

SERVES 8

12 ounces (340g) gingersnaps (about 48 cookies)

½ cup (110g) unsalted butter, at room temperature and cut into several large pieces

3 or 4 Granny Smith apples

1 cup (200g) brown sugar

2 tablespoons all-purpose flour

¼ teaspoon kosher salt

1 teaspoon ground cinnamon

½ teaspoon ground ginger

¼ teaspoon ground cloves

Juice and finely grated zest of 1 lemon

You'd be hard-pressed to find an apple dessert that's simpler (or more delicious) than a brown betty, which is made by simply layering buttery breadcrumbs with sweetened apples and baking until toasty and golden. This version improves upon the time-honored formula by replacing the breadcrumbs with gingersnap crumbs. As the betty bubbles in the oven, your whole kitchen will start to smell like autumn; when it's finished, you'll have the ideal mixture of soft, baked apples and crunchy, spiced cookie crumbs.

1. Preheat the oven to 350°F (175°C).

2. Put the gingersnaps in a food processor and grind them into small pieces. Add the butter and process until evenly combined.

3. Peel and core the apples, then slice them very thinly. Put them in a large bowl. Add the brown sugar, flour, salt, cinnamon, ginger, and cloves and stir gently until well combined. Add the lemon juice and zest and gently stir again until the apples are evenly coated.

4. Put one-third of the crumb mixture in a deep 9-inch (23cm) pie plate and spread it evenly over the bottom. Layer half of the apples on top of the crumbs. Scatter another one-third of the crumbs evenly over the apples, then arrange the remaining apples on top. Spread the remaining crumbs evenly over the apples so that they are completely covered.

5. Bake for 30 to 40 minutes, until the apples are soft and the crumb topping is crunchy. Let cool for at least 15 minutes before serving.

Almond Butter and Oatmeal Crisp

SERVES 8 TO 10

Pears

1 tablespoon cornstarch

1 to 4 tablespoons raw sugar, to taste

¼ teaspoon ground cinnamon

¼ teaspoon freshly grated nutmeg

Small pinch of ground cloves

3 pounds (1.4 kg) ripe pears (7 or 10 medium pears)

⅓ cup (40g) dried cranberries

Topping

6 tablespoons (95g) almond butter

1 tablespoon raw sugar

¼ teaspoon ground cinnamon

¼ teaspoon freshly grated nutmeg

1 tablespoon coconut oil or melted butter

2 teaspoons vanilla extract

Scant ¼ teaspoon almond extract

Small pinch of sea salt

1¼ cups (115g) rolled oats

¾ cup almonds (105g) or walnuts or pecans (about 80g), toasted and coarsely chopped

¼ cup (60ml) cream (or almond milk whisked with 1 teaspoon cornstarch)

Food52er Helen Conroy (aka AntoniaJames) had the brilliant idea to bake a nutty, chewy cookie until it's barely done, break it up into chunks, and use it to top a spiced mixture of fall fruits. The result is the crunchiest, most wholesome crisp we've tasted yet.

---

1. Put one shelf in the lower third of the oven and another shelf in the upper third. Preheat the oven to 375°F (190°C). Have a large, shallow baking pan on hand; 9 by 13 inches (23 by 33cm) works nicely.

2. To prepare the pear filling, stir together the cornstarch, sugar (the quantity depends on the sweetness of your pears), cinnamon, nutmeg, and cloves in a small bowl.

3. Peel, core, and chop the pears into ½-inch (1.3cm) pieces, putting the chunks in the baking pan as you cut them. Sprinkle with the cornstarch-sugar-spice mixture, add the dried cranberries, and toss gently until the pears are evenly coated. Cover tightly with aluminum foil and set aside.

4. Next, make the topping. Line a baking sheet that's larger than the baking dish with parchment paper. In a large bowl, combine the almond butter, sugar, cinnamon, nutmeg, coconut oil, vanilla and almond extracts, and salt. Stir in the rolled oats and nuts. Transfer the crumble to the baking sheet and pat it into an even layer about the size of the baking pan.

5. Put the baking sheet in the oven on the upper shelf and put the pears on the bottom shelf. Bake for 12 minutes. Remove both the cookie and the pears from the oven but leave the oven on. Use the edge of a spatula to break the giant cookie into uneven pieces about 2 inches (5cm) across. Uncover the pears, drizzle the cream over them, then cover them with the cookie pieces.

6. Bake uncovered for 20 to 25 minutes, checking after 15 minutes to make sure the topping isn't getting too dark. If needed, cover with the foil for the last 5 to 10 minutes of baking. Let cool for at least 5 minutes before serving.

Blueberry Cream Torte

SERVES 8

Blueberry Topping

4 cups (600g) blueberries

1/2 cup (120ml) water

1/4 cup (30g) confectioners' sugar

1 teaspoon freshly squeezed lemon juice

Crust

1 cup (85g) graham cracker crumbs (about 12 graham cracker squares)

1 cup (125g) all-purpose flour

3/4 cup (170g) unsalted butter, melted

1 cup (100g) walnuts, coarsely chopped

Filling

8 ounces (225g) cream cheese, at room temperature

1 1/2 cups (185g) confectioners' sugar

2 cups (475ml) heavy cream

This impressive dessert is like a blueberry pie emptied onto a cheesecake, while managing to be lighter and prettier than either. Calling it a torte is meant to make it seem fancy (it sounds a lot better than "no-bake cheesecake"), but it was originally a dinner party dessert that executive editor Kristen Miglore's mother could throw together in 30 minutes. Her version called for canned blueberry pie filling and, when there wasn't cream in the house, a packet of Dream Whip. Kristen updated the recipe so that even the blueberry layer is made from scratch. Though it may seem like this adds unnecessary hassle, it's not always easy to find good-quality canned blueberry pie filling, so making your own might actually save you some work.

---

1. Preheat the oven to 350°F (175°C).

2. To make the topping, put 2 cups (300g) of the blueberries in a small saucepan, selecting the softest, ripest berries of the bunch. Stir in the water and confectioners' sugar and bring to a simmer over medium-low heat. Adjust the heat to maintain a simmer and cook, stirring and mashing the berries occasionally with a wooden spoon, until they break down completely and the juices thickly coat the back of the spoon, about 15 minutes.

3. Strain through a fine-mesh sieve, pushing the mixture through with a silicone or rubber spatula and scraping the bottom of the strainer to get every last delicious drop. You should have about 1 cup (240ml) of blueberry sauce. Fold in the remaining 2 cups (300g) of blueberries. Stir in the lemon juice, then taste and add more confectioners' sugar or lemon juice if needed. Let cool completely (if you're in a hurry, you can chill the topping in the freezer).

4. To make the crust, put the graham cracker crumbs and flour in a food processor. With the processor running, pour in the melted butter. Add the walnuts and pulse quickly a couple of times to combine, but be sure to leave the nuts a bit chunky. Press the mixture evenly into the bottom (not up the sides) of a 9- or 10-inch (23 or 25cm) round springform pan. Bake for 10 to 15 minutes, until the crust is dry and a shade darker. Let cool completely, about an hour (chill the crust in the freezer if you're in a rush).

CONTINUED

5. Meanwhile, make the filling. Using an electric mixer or creaming vigorously with a wooden spoon, beat the cream cheese with the confectioners' sugar until completely smooth.

6. Put the cream in a cold, clean bowl. Using an electric mixer fitted with the whisk attachment or whisking vigorously by hand, whip until stiff peaks form (see page 106). Fold the whipped cream into the cream cheese mixture.

7. To assemble the torte, spread the filling carefully over the cooled crust, smoothing it out with a spatula. Spoon the cooled blueberry topping evenly over the filling; the topping will probably come right to the top of the pan. Refrigerate in the pan for at least 6 hours or up to 1 day.

8. To serve, set the pan on a serving platter. Run a knife around the edge of the pan to loosen the torte, then remove the outer ring. The blueberry topping will flow down over the edges of the torte—more so if the torte isn't well chilled. Serve immediately, and refrigerate any leftovers.

How to Quickly Cool a Small Batch of Liquid

If you ever need to cool down a small batch of hot liquid fast—an ice cream base, custard, or even this blueberry sauce—use an ice bath. Pour the hot liquid into a metal Bundt pan that's nested in a large bowl of ice water. The metal helps conduct the heat out (and the cold in) quickly, and the hole in the middle of the pan creates more surface area, which means more rapid chilling.

Summary Fruit Galette

MAKES ONE 10-INCH (25CM) GALETTE; SERVES 6 TO 8

Crust

½ cup (110g) salted butter

½ cup (60g) whole wheat flour

¾ cup (95g) all-purpose flour

½ teaspoon salt

2 to 3 tablespoons ice water

1 tablespoon apple cider vinegar

Filling

2 pounds (900g) plums or other fruit, thinly sliced

⅓ cup (65g) sugar, preferably raw sugar

1 heaping tablespoon all-purpose flour

Pinch of salt

Zest of 1 lemon, finely grated (optional)

Dash of vanilla extract (optional)

Pinch of ground cinnamon (optional)

1 egg, beaten

Flaky salt, for sprinkling

Raw sugar, for sprinkling

If pie is for people who wake up with the sun, ready to take on the world, then galette is for those of us who mosey out of bed at 10 a.m. As former editor Marian Bull puts it, "A galette is a lazy woman's pie. A galette is a happy woman's pie." There's no fussing over latticework or crimped edges. In fact, the less perfect your galette looks, the more beautifully rustic it will be. Plus, you can make this free-form fruit tart with whatever ripe fruit you have on hand; summer stone fruit works especially well. Learn this dough recipe by heart. It's wholesome and savory enough to be the base for a vegetable galette too, as in the Savory Galette with Greens and Gruyère (page 138).

---

1. To make the crust, cut the butter into ½-inch (1.3cm) pieces, put it on a plate, and freeze for 5 to 10 minutes, until the butter is firm but not overly hard.

2. In a medium bowl, stir together the flours and salt with a fork or whisk. Add half of the butter to the flour mixture and toss to coat; ideally, you want a flour barrier between your hands and the butter at all times. Cut in the butter with a pastry cutter or by hand, using a snapping motion with your fingers, until the mixture is crumbly. Add the remaining butter, toss to coat, and cut in again, this time pressing the butter into flat sheets, which will make the crust flakier. Stop when all of the butter is either in small pieces the size of peas or lima beans or in small, flat sheets.

3. Combine 2 tablespoons of the ice water with the vinegar, then sprinkle over the flour mixture a tablespoonful at a time, tossing lightly to distribute the liquid evenly through the flour. Stop when the ingredients just come together and a bit of dough holds together when you squeeze it. If it's crumbly, add a bit more water, just a little at a time.

4. Form the dough into a ball, then pat it into a fat disk. Wrap tightly in plastic wrap and refrigerate for 3 to 12 hours (or freeze for up to 3 weeks). If freezing the dough, let it thaw overnight in the refrigerator before rolling it out.

CONTINUED

5. To make the filling, shortly before you plan to bake the galette, preheat the oven to 425°F (220°C). Toss all the ingredients together until the plums are evenly coated. Let sit for about 15 minutes, then drain off the juices.

6. To assemble and bake the galette, put the dough on a floured work surface and flour the top of the dough and a rolling pin while the filling sits. Roll out the dough to form a rough circle about 14 inches (36cm) in diameter and ¼ inch (6mm) thick. Keep rotating the dough as you roll it out so it doesn't stick to the work surface, and sprinkle the dough and work surface with flour as needed to prevent sticking.

7. Line a baking sheet with parchment paper, then transfer the dough to the lined baking sheet by curling it around the rolling pin and then unfurling it. If it's soft, pop it in the fridge for a few minutes to firm up.

8. Transfer the plums to fine-mesh sieve and give it a few assertive shakes to drain off any excess moisture. Pile the plums in the center of the dough, leaving a 2-inch (5cm) bare edge around the circumference. Fold small sections of the edges of the dough over the filling to seal your galette. If the dough is feeling particularly soft, stick the whole pan in the refrigerator or freezer to firm up, 10 to 20 minutes. Brush the egg evenly over the crust and then sprinkle the crust with flaky salt and raw sugar.

9. Bake for 35 to 40 minutes, until the crust is a deep golden brown, with no pale areas, and feels dry and flaky. Let cool until the filling sets up before slicing and serving.

How to Cut in Butter

Cutting butter into flour ensures that the butter is incorporated into the dry ingredients in small, intact chunks that will melt and steam in the oven to create a flaky crust. When cutting in butter, make sure the butter is cold. It's even helpful to cube the butter and put it in the freezer to chill, along with the bowl and any other tools you're using. Dump the cold, cubed butter into the flour or other dry ingredients and use a pastry blender, a fork, or your fingers to break it up into smaller pieces. If using your fingers, work quickly so the heat of your hands doesn't warm the butter excessively. Toss the butter and flour together, pressing down on the butter and smashing any big chunks into smaller pieces. Stop when the flour is lumpy with lima bean– or pea-size pieces of butter.

Peach Tart

MAKES ONE 11-INCH (28CM) TART; SERVES 8

Crust

1½ cups (190g) all-purpose flour

1 teaspoon sugar

½ teaspoon kosher salt

¼ cup (60ml) vegetable oil or canola oil

¼ cup (60ml) mild olive oil

2 tablespoons whole milk

½ teaspoon almond extract

Filling

¾ cup (150g) sugar

2 to 3 tablespoons all-purpose flour

¼ teaspoon kosher salt

2 tablespoons cold unsalted butter

3 to 5 small, ripe peaches, or 5 ripe plums, pitted and sliced ½ inch (1.3cm) thick

Every cook needs a good dessert recipe that can be whipped up anywhere— especially when you're away from your kitchen and its familiar gadgets. This is that recipe. To make it, all you need is a knife, a bowl, and some kind of pan—a tart pan, ideally. When you're without a bowl, you can mix the dough right in the pan, and when you're without peaches, you can substitute another ripe stone fruit. For added indulgence, top each serving with a dollop of whipped cream.

---

1. Preheat the oven to 425°F (220°C). To make the crust, stir together the flour, sugar, and salt in a bowl.

2. In a small bowl, whisk together the oils, milk, and almond extract. Pour into the flour mixture and stir gently with a fork, being careful to not overwork the dough.

3. Place the dough in the center of an 11-inch (28cm) tart pan. Pinch off small pieces and use them to cover the sides of the pan first, then press the rest of the mound of dough outward to the sides. Use the entire pads of your fingers, rather than just the tips, so the dough reaches the edges. It should be about ⅛ inch (3mm) thick all around. Trim and discard any excess dough.

4. To make the filling, combine the sugar, 2 tablespoons of the flour, the salt, and butter in a small bowl. (If the peaches are especially juicy, add another 1 tablespoon of flour.) Using your fingertips, pinch the butter into the sugar mixture until crumbly; the texture should include both fine granules and small pebbly bits.

5. Starting along the outside edge of the tart crust, arrange the peaches, slightly overlapping, in concentric circles. The peaches should fit snugly. Sprinkle the sugar mixture over the peaches.

6. Bake for 35 to 45 minutes, until shiny, thick bubbles begin enveloping the fruit and the crust is slightly brown. Put the pan on a rack and let cool at least briefly. Serve warm or at room temperature.

"Cuppa Cuppa Sticka" Peach and Blueberry Cobbler

SERVES 6 TO 8

1 cup (125g) self-rising flour

1 cup (200g) sugar

Pinch of salt

1 cup (240ml) whole milk

1 teaspoon vanilla extract

½ cup (110g) unsalted butter

4 peaches, chopped into bite-size pieces (about 2 cups/480ml)

¼ cup (40g) blueberries

Not a traditional two-layer cobbler with fruit on the bottom and a crumble or biscuit on the top, this summer treat is instead, in the words of Kate Williams, the freelance writer and personal chef who created this recipe, a "supremely buttery and moist cake studded with fruit." Melting the butter directly in the pan instead of mixing it into the batter creates crisp, browned edges and a moist, custardy center—a dish that's part buckle, part clafoutis, and 100 percent unique. And the name? It comes from the fact that "there's a 'cuppa' self-rising flour, a 'cuppa' milk, a 'cuppa' sugar, and a 'sticka' butter in addition to the fruit and a little vanilla. (It should really have three 'cuppas' in the name)." While it's a wonderful dessert, especially with a scoop of vanilla ice cream, you might also serve it at brunch alongside scrambled eggs and fresh juice.

———

1. Preheat the oven to 350°F (175°C).

2. In a large bowl, whisk together the flour, sugar, and salt. Add the milk and vanilla and whisk gently until as smooth as possible (a couple of tiny lumps are okay).

3. Put the butter in a 9 by 13-inch (23 by 33cm) baking pan and set it in the oven to melt. Once the butter has melted and is starting to bubble, remove the pan from the oven and rotate it to evenly coat the bottom and sides with the butter.

4. Pour the batter into the hot pan and use a spatula to spread it evenly. Butter will slosh over the sides of the batter; this is a good thing. Scatter the peaches and blueberries evenly over the top.

5. Bake for 35 to 40 minutes, until the center is just set and the edges are deep golden brown.

6. Serve the cobbler hot, warm, or at room temperature, or even cold from the fridge.

Custardy Cakes
& Puddings

Challah Bread Pudding "Soufflé"

MAKES ONE 9 BY 13-INCH (23 BY 33CM) "SOUFFLÉ"; SERVES 12 TO 15

1 large loaf of challah (plain or with raisins), sliced 1 inch (2.5cm) thick

8 eggs, lightly beaten

3 cups (710ml) milk

1 tablespoon vanilla extract

½ cup (100g) sugar, plus more for sprinkling

½ cup (75g) raisins (optional)

Ground cinnamon

Caramel or vanilla ice cream, for serving

Soufflé is for those who like to live on the wild side. Though it can be the star of the party, it's unreliable and—here comes the punch line—it may let you down. So if you're looking for a dessert you can count on—something you can turn to when the priority is feeding a lot of people rather than putting on a show—make this "soufflé" instead. Assemble it the day or morning before a party. Then, while dinner is on the table, put it in the oven, where it will puff and inflate like a sail catching the wind. If it deflates a little when you take it out of the oven, there's no harm done; it will still taste fantastic. For entertaining, you might want to use a pretty casserole dish that you can bring directly to the table from the oven.

1. Butter a 9 by 13-inch (23 by 33cm) baking pan.

2. Fit all of the challah slices into the prepared pan. No need to get fancy— just smoosh it all in.

3. In a large bowl, whisk together the eggs, milk, vanilla, and sugar. Stir in the raisins, then pour the mixture evenly over the challah. Sprinkle cinnamon and sugar evenly over the top. Cover tightly and refrigerate for 4 to 36 hours (overnight is best). When you're ready to bake, preheat the oven to 350°F (175°C).

4. Remove the wrapping from your baking pan and replace it with a generous amount of aluminum foil, tenting it so it doesn't touch the surface as the "soufflé" rises. Bake for 40 to 50 minutes, until puffy and golden brown under the foil.

5. Serve the "soufflé" immediately (it will fall quickly as it cools), with ice cream alongside.

Raspberry Clafoutis

SERVES 6

2 tablespoons unsalted butter, melted

1 cup (240ml) half-and-half

2 eggs

1 egg yolk

¾ cup (150g) granulated sugar, preferably vanilla sugar (see tip below)

¼ teaspoon almond extract (optional)

½ cup (60g) all-purpose flour

1½ cups (190g) fresh raspberries

Confectioners' sugar, for dusting

When you're graced with beautiful, flavorful raspberries, don't hide them in a crisp or a crumble. Instead, float them on a pool of light, creamy custard where they can be admired. Clafoutis is a cross between a tart and a flan—with set, brown edges and a jiggly, gooey center—yet it's less intimidating to make than either. Try whipping up clafoutis when you're in the mood for pot de crème or crème brûlée. It's slightly sweet, slightly eggy, and very French sounding.

---

1. Preheat the oven to 325°F (165°C). Brush a 9-inch (23cm) pie plate with the melted butter.

2. In a large bowl, whisk together the half-and-half, eggs, egg yolk, vanilla sugar, and almond extract. Add the flour and whisk just until smooth, being careful not to overmix. Pour the batter into the prepared pie plate and scatter the raspberries evenly over the top.

3. Bake for 30 to 35 minutes, until the clafoutis is just set and the surface is golden brown. Dust with confectioners' sugar and serve warm.

How to Make Scented Sugar at Home

To give this dessert a lovely, subtle vanilla flavor, try baking with vanilla-scented sugar: with a butter knife, scrape the seeds out of half of a vanilla bean that's been cut lengthwise; then, use your fingers to rub the seeds into the sugar until it's speckled and fragrant. Keep any extra vanilla sugar on hand for anytime you want to add a special touch to your baked goods.

Pudding Chômeur

SERVES 10 TO 12

2/3 cup (150g) unsalted butter

1 cup (200g) sugar

2 eggs

2 1/3 cups (290g) all-purpose flour

1 teaspoon baking powder

2 cups (475ml) maple syrup

2 cups (475ml) heavy cream

Whipped cream, for serving

If you were to cross sticky toffee pudding with pancakes and maple syrup, you'd get *pouding chômeur*, a buttery biscuit submerged in a bath of maple syrup and cream. This French-Canadian confection, with a name that translates to "unemployed person's pudding," is made from ingredients that were inexpensive and abundant when the recipe was first created in Québec. It's easy to prepare: you can mix the dough in just 10 minutes. Then, after chilling it for a day, all you have to do is drop the dough into ramekins, pour the syrup and cream overtop, and bake. As the liquid boils in the oven, it poaches and glazes the dough. It's an impressive no-stress dessert to serve at a dinner party for 10, but if you prefer bigger portions, bake the pudding in 6 large ramekins and increase the baking time to 25 minutes.

---

1. Using a stand mixer fitted with a paddle attachment or a handheld electric mixer, beat the butter and sugar until smooth. Add the eggs one at a time, mixing well after each addition and scraping down the sides of the bowl occasionally. Add the flour and baking powder and stir until completely incorporated. Cover the bowl tightly and refrigerate for at least 24 hours and up to 36 hours.

2. About 1 hour before you plan to serve the pudding, preheat the oven to 450°F (230°C).

3. Combine the maple syrup and cream in a saucepan over medium-high heat and bring to a boil, stirring occasionally. Immediately remove from the heat.

4. Divide the dough among ten to twelve small (4-ounce/120ml) ramekins; it should fill the ramekins about halfway. Pour in the syrup mixture, dividing it evenly among the ramekins, but make sure it doesn't come any closer than 1/2 inch (1.3cm) from the rim; any fuller and it will boil over.

5. Put the ramekins on a baking sheet and bake for about 20 minutes, until the sauce is bubbling and a tester inserted into the center comes out clean. Serve warm with whipped cream.

Baked Rice Pudding with Coconut Milk and Honey

SERVES 8 TO 10

Pudding

⅓ cup (65g) medium-grain white rice

2 (13½-ounce/378ml) cans full-fat coconut milk

½ cup (120ml) honey

2 teaspoons vanilla extract

½ teaspoon ground nutmeg

Generous pinch of salt

Topping

½ cup (40g) unsweetened dried coconut flakes

½ cup (45g) sliced almonds

3 medjool dates, pitted

Generous pinch of ground nutmeg

Small pinch of salt

Creamy and soothing rice pudding is as enjoyable eaten warm in front of a fire as it is eaten cold for breakfast the next morning. But this isn't your typical rendition; it's made in the oven, not on top of the stove, and it uses coconut milk rather than dairy, which gives it a rich, almost tropical taste. Because you can let the pudding do its own thing in the oven, you'll have plenty of time to put together the coconut-date topping, which, by the way, is just as good on oatmeal or yogurt as it is on this dessert.

---

1. Preheat the oven to 300°F (150°C). Butter a deep baking dish measuring about 2 quarts (2 L)—the exact size doesn't matter.

2. To make the pudding, stir together all of the ingredients in a bowl, then pour into the prepared baking dish.

3. Bake for 30 minutes, then stir. Repeat this two more times, stirring at the end of each 30-minute interval. Toward the end of this time, the pudding will begin to thicken and look like, well, pudding. After the third time you stir, at 90 minutes, start stirring at 10-minute intervals. Each time, check the consistency by letting a bit of the pudding cool slightly on the back of a spoon and then drawing a finger through it. The pudding is done when it looks thick and creamy and the track from your finger remains. Continue to bake and stir at 10-minute intervals until the pudding is done. The total baking time may be up to 2 hours.

4. Meanwhile, prepare the topping. Toast the coconut and almonds together in a dry skillet over medium heat, stirring often, until golden. Let cool a bit.

5. Coarsely chop the dates, then put them in a food processor. Add the coconut, almonds, nutmeg, and salt and pulse until the mixture has a coarse crumbly texture; alternatively, you can finely chop everything by hand.

6. Serve the rice pudding warm or cold, topped with the coconut mixture. If cooling the pudding, stir it occasionally as it cools to prevent a skin from forming.

Lemon Sponge Cups

SERVES 4 TO 6

2 tablespoons unsalted butter, at room temperature

1 cup (200g) sugar

¼ cup (30g) all-purpose flour

Finely grated zest and juice of 1 lemon

Pinch of salt

3 eggs, separated

1½ cups (355ml) milk

Thin slices of lemon, for garnish

This is what to make when you're in need of something that's just the right amount of impressive. A twist on a classic lemon pudding cake, these sponge cups are a little like a layman's soufflé, using some similar processes like beating the separated eggs for the batter and baking the cups in a water bath. When these little light-as-air cakes—each in a pool of lemony custard—come out of the oven, you'll feel accomplished. You'll know they were a breeze to make, but no one else has to.

1. Preheat the oven to 350°F (175°C).

2. Put the butter, sugar, flour, lemon zest and juice, and salt in a large bowl. Using an electric mixer or creaming vigorously with a wooden spoon, beat until well combined. Scrape down the sides of the bowl to make sure everything is thoroughly mixed.

3. In a separate medium bowl, whisk the egg yolks. Add the milk and whisk until smooth. Gradually stir into the butter-sugar mixture, whisking by hand as you pour.

4. Put the egg whites in a clean, dry bowl. Using an electric mixer fitted with the whisk attachment or whisking vigorously by hand, whip until stiff peaks form (see page 106). Gently fold the egg whites into the sugar mixture. Since the sugar mixture is loose and liquidy, your batter might be a bit lumpy after folding in the egg whites—do not be alarmed.

5. Pour the mixture into four to six ramekins or individual soufflé dishes. Put them in baking pan and pour in enough hot water to reach about halfway up the sides of the ramekins.

6. Bake for 45 minutes; when done, the sponge cups will be lightly browned on top, with a layer of lemon custard beneath.

7. Let cool slightly before serving, either in the ramekins or turned out onto serving plates. Garnish with a slice of lemon.

Sour Cream Cheesecake with Chocolate Cookie Crust

MAKES ONE 9-INCH (23CM) CHEESECAKE; SERVES 10 TO 12

Crust

1½ cups (165g) chocolate cookie crumbs

¼ teaspoon ground cinnamon

¼ cup (60g) salted butter, melted

Filling

16 ounces (450g) cream cheese, at room temperature

2 eggs

⅔ cup (135g) sugar

2 teaspoons vanilla extract

Topping

1½ cups (355ml) sour cream

¼ cup (50g) sugar

2 teaspoons vanilla extract

This cheesecake, which comes to us from Amanda's mother, Judy, has a dual personality—a silky, tangy sour cream layer atop a traditional cheesecake. Amanda describes this dessert as "a middlebrow cheesecake with highbrow aspirations." Don't be intimidated by the fact that there's more than one layer here; even though this cheesecake has more complex flavors and textures than your usual suspect, it's just as easy to make.

The top shouldn't crack—if it does, take the cheesecake out of the oven sooner the next time you make it. By the way, for the chocolate cookie crumbs in the crust, we recommend Nabisco's Famous Chocolate Wafers.

---

1. Preheat the oven to 350°F (175°C).

2. To make the crust, put the cookie crumbs, cinnamon, and butter in a medium bowl and mix until the crumbs are evenly moist. Transfer the mixture to a 9-inch (23cm) round springform pan and press it evenly across the bottom and about 1 inch (2.5cm) up the sides.

3. To make the filling, put the cream cheese in a large bowl. Using an electric mixer or stirring vigorously with a wooden spoon, beat until soft and creamy. Add the eggs, sugar, and vanilla and beat until very smooth.

4. Carefully pour the filling over the crust and smooth the top with a rubber spatula. Bake for 25 minutes, until the filling is set enough to jiggle when gently shaken and the edges look slightly puffed and golden.

5. Meanwhile, make the topping, stirring together the sour cream, sugar, and vanilla until smooth.

6. After the cheesecake has baked for 25 minutes, remove it from the oven and turn the oven temperature up to 450°F (230°C). Gently spread the sour cream mixture over the filling, then return the cheesecake to the oven and bake for 7 minutes longer. Let cool completely before slicing and serving. Serve chilled or at room temperature.

Coconut Tres Leches Cake

MAKES ONE 9 BY 13-INCH (23 BY 33CM) CAKE; SERVES 10 TO 12

Cake
½ cup (110g) unsalted butter

1 tablespoon honey

1¼ cups (155g) all-purpose flour

¼ cup (30g) coconut flour

1 teaspoon baking powder

½ teaspoon salt

5 eggs

¾ cup sugar

1 teaspoon vanilla extract

Soaking Mixture
1 (13½-ounce/378ml) can coconut milk

1 (14-ounce/397g) can sweetened condensed milk

1½ cups (355ml) whole milk

Toppings
1 cup (95g) sweetened shredded dried coconut

2 cups (475ml) heavy cream

2 tablespoons sugar

Zest of 1 lime, finely grated

When we made this in our test kitchen, our entire staff kept returning to the pan until, scoop by scoop, the enormous cake was gone. The amount of liquid this cake soaks up almost defies the laws of science. It's rich and, yes, moist—and probably the coconuttiest dessert you've ever had. The lime adds a citrusy brightness that helps keep the dish from being too sweet or too heavy.

1. Preheat the oven to 350°F (175°C). Butter a 9 by 13-inch (23 by 33cm) baking pan.

2. To make the cake, combine the butter and honey in a small saucepan over medium-low heat and cook, stirring occasionally, until the butter is melted. In a medium bowl, whisk together the flours, baking powder, and salt.

3. Using an electric mixer or stirring vigorously by hand, beat the eggs, sugar, and vanilla in a large bowl until smooth and lighter in color. Turn the mixer down to low speed and add the flour mixture in two additions, mixing just until the batter is smooth. Fold in the butter mixture just until incorporated. Pour the batter into the prepared pan.

4. Bake for 15 minutes, then rotate the pan and bake for 10 to 15 minutes longer, until the top is golden and a toothpick inserted into the center comes out clean.

5. Prepare the soaking mixture by mixing the three milks together. Use a toothpick to poke holes all over the top of the warm cake. Leaving the cake in the pan, slowly pour the soaking mixture over it. It's going to look like a lot of milk, and the cake may even float up briefly. Don't panic! The cake will absorb about 95 percent of that milk. Let cool completely.

6. While the cake soaks, to prepare the toppings: spread the coconut on a rimmed baking sheet. When the cake is baked, pop the coconut into the oven. Check on it and stir every 3 to 4 minutes; it should be toasted in 8 to 9 minutes.

7. Meanwhile, put the cream, sugar, and lime zest in a cold bowl. Using an electric mixer fitted with the whisk attachment or whisking vigorously, whip until stiff peaks form (see page 106). Spread the whipped cream over the cake, then sprinkle the cooled coconut over the top. Serve immediately, or cover and refrigerate for up to 4 days.

Everyday Cakes

Strawberry-Yogurt Snack Cake

MAKES ONE 8 BY 12-INCH (20 BY 30CM) CAKE; SERVES 8 TO 12

2 cups (250g) all-purpose flour

2 teaspoons baking powder

½ teaspoon kosher salt

1 cup (240ml) plain Greek yogurt, at room temperature

½ cup (120ml) milk, at room temperature

½ cup (110g) unsalted butter, at room temperature

1 cup (200g) granulated sugar

2 teaspoons vanilla extract

2 tablespoons vegetable oil

2 eggs, at room temperature

1½ pounds (680g) strawberries, halved

2 tablespoons raw sugar, for sprinkling

Plush with fruit and tangy from yogurt, this is a cake for committing to memory. It's a snack cake, which means you can eat it when you please, pack it up for lunch, and saw off slices when you pass it in the kitchen. Its pretty top—a mosaic of bright fruit and golden cake—makes it suitable to serve to guests (and perfect for Mother's Day). If strawberries are not your favorite, substitute stone fruits such as apricots, plums, or nectarines. Simply pit and chop them into strawberry-sized pieces before using.

---

1. Preheat the oven to 350°F (175°C). Butter an 8 by 12-inch (20 by 30cm) ceramic baking dish or a 9-inch (23cm) circular cake pan 2 inches (5cm) in height.

2. In a medium bowl, whisk together the flour, baking powder, and salt until thoroughly blended. In a small bowl, whisk the yogurt and milk together. Set both aside.

3. Using a stand mixer fitted with the paddle attachment or a handheld electric mixer, beat the butter on medium speed until very pale in color, about 3 minutes. Add the granulated sugar and beat for 3 minutes longer, until almost white, scraping down the sides of the bowl as needed. Add the vanilla and oil and beat until well blended.

4. Turn the mixer down to medium-low speed and add the eggs one at a time, mixing just until well blended after each addition. Turn the mixer down to its lowest setting and add the yogurt mixture and flour mixture in several alternating additions, mixing just until blended after each addition and scraping down the sides of the bowl occasionally.

5. Pour the batter into the buttered baking dish and smooth the top. Place the strawberries on the top in a pretty pattern, cut side down. Sprinkle with the turbinado sugar.

6. Bake for about 1 hour and 10 minutes, until the edges are golden brown and a toothpick inserted into the center comes out clean.

7. Cool completely in the pan. When ready to serve, invert the cake onto a plate or wire rack, then top with the serving plate and invert again so that the strawberries are visible when served.

Easy-as-Pie Apple Cake

MAKES ONE 9-INCH (23CM) ROUND CAKE; SERVES 8

1 cup (125g) all-purpose flour

¼ teaspoon baking soda

¼ teaspoon kosher salt

¼ cup (60g) unsalted butter,
at room temperature

1 cup (200g) sugar

1 teaspoon vanilla extract

1 teaspoon ground cinnamon

¼ teaspoon freshly grated
nutmeg

1 egg

2 cups (300g) diced apples

½ cup (60g) toasted pecans
(optional), chopped

We wouldn't dare deny the timeless perfection of apple pie. But when we find ourselves in the midst of autumn and up to our eyes in pie, this cake is a worthy option. It's perfect for post-Thanksgiving fatigue, when we're still in the mood for dessert but not in the mood to roll out dough or peel lots of apples. And just like apple pie, it's delicious with a spoonful of whipped cream, a dollop of crème fraîche, or a scoop of good vanilla ice cream. As a bonus, this light, chewy cake comes together so quickly that you could even make it in time for breakfast.

1. Preheat the oven to 350°F (175°C). Butter and flour a 9-inch (23cm) fluted tart pan with a removable bottom or a 9-inch (23cm) round cake pan with 1-inch (2.5cm) sides; if using a cake pan, line the bottom with parchment paper, as well.

2. In a small bowl, whisk together the flour, baking soda, and salt.

3. Using an electric mixer or creaming vigorously with a wooden spoon, beat the butter, sugar, vanilla, cinnamon, and nutmeg until pale in color and fluffy. Add the egg and mix until smooth. Add the flour mixture and mix again until smooth; the batter will be thick. Stir in the apples and pecans. Transfer the batter to the prepared pan and spread it evenly.

4. Bake for 40 to 45 minutes, until a toothpick inserted into the center comes out clean and the top is a nice golden color.

5. Let cool slightly. If you used a tart pan with a removable bottom, nudge the cake out carefully while it is still a bit warm. If you used a cake pan, let cool slightly, then run a thin knife around the edge of the pan; turn out onto a plate or wire rack, then invert onto a cake plate so the crispy top of the cake is facing up.

Cold-Oven Pound Cake

MAKES 1 TUBE CAKE; SERVES 10 TO 12

1 cup (225g) salted butter, cubed

½ cup (100g) solid shortening

3 cups (600g) sugar

5 eggs, separated

1 teaspoon vanilla extract

1 cup (240ml) reduced-fat milk, 2% or less

3 cups (375g) all-purpose flour

A perfect pound cake is a magical thing: a go-to cake for all occasions made with ingredients you probably keep on hand. This recipe comes to us from Food52er Muffinj, who got it from her grandmother. Like all great old-fashioned recipes, it once lived on a splotched and well-worn index card that has since been lost. We're so thankful that the recipe lives on in a different form.

It produces a beautiful cake with a crunchy, caramelized exterior and a dense, creamy-textured interior. It's great on its own, and even better when served with ice cream, macerated strawberries, or lemon curd. But don't stop there: try toasting or griddling thick slices, or cut the cake into chunks and dip them into fondue. Perhaps this cake really is magical; Muffinj's friends swear it cures whatever illness they have at the moment.

---

1. Butter and flour a tube or Bundt pan.

2. Using a stand mixer fitted with a paddle attachment or a handheld electric mixer, beat the butter, shortening, and sugar until light and fluffy. Add the egg yolks and beat until incorporated.

3. Stir the vanilla into the milk, then pour ⅓ cup (80ml) of the milk into the sugar mixture. Add 1 cup (125g) of the flour and beat just until incorporated; don't overmix. Repeat the process, adding the milk and flour in two more additions, beating just until incorporated each time.

4. Put the egg whites in a clean, dry bowl. Using an electric mixer with the whisk attachment or whisking vigorously by hand, whip until stiff peaks form (see page 106). Gently fold the egg whites into the batter. Pour the batter into the prepared pan and put the pan in a cold oven.

5. Turn the oven on to 300°F (150°C) and bake the cake for 45 minutes. Raise the temperature to 325°F (165°C) and bake for 45 minutes longer, until the cake is golden and a toothpick inserted into the middle comes out clean.

6. Put the pan on a wire rack and let cool for 20 minutes. Run a knife around the edge and, if you used a tube pan, invert the cake onto the wire rack, and then invert it onto a serving plate; if you used a Bundt pan, simply invert it from the pan onto a serving plate.

Honey Pecan Cake

MAKES ONE 9-INCH (23CM) ROUND CAKE; SERVES 6 TO 8

Topping

2 tablespoons unsalted butter

¼ cup (60ml) honey

Generous pinch of salt

1 cup (100g) pecan halves

Cake

½ cup (50g) pecan halves

1 cup (125g) all-purpose flour

1 teaspoon baking powder

½ teaspoon salt

3 eggs, separated

½ cup (110g) unsalted butter, at room temperature

½ cup (100g) sugar

¼ cup honey

1 teaspoon vanilla extract

½ cup (120ml) buttermilk

This cake uses precious pecans in two ways: first, cooked into a crunchy, sticky layer that becomes the topping of the cake, and second, pulverized into a flour that brings the entire dessert together. This impressive-looking cake could grace your dinner party table, but is simple enough that you can (and should) make it for no special reason, too. Save yourself a piece for breakfast the next day.

---

1. Preheat the oven to 350°F (175°C). Butter a 9-inch (23cm) round cake pan, then line the bottom with parchment paper, making sure there are no gaps between the pan and the paper. Place it on a baking sheet.

2. To make the topping, combine the butter, honey, and salt in a small saucepan over medium-low heat and cook, stirring often, until the butter has melted. Pour into the prepared pan, then sprinkle on the pecans.

3. To make the cake, put the pecans in a food processor and pulse to make pecan flour (see page 95). Transfer to a medium bowl, add the flour, baking powder, and salt, and whisk to combine.

4. Put the egg whites in a clean, dry bowl. Using an electric mixer fitted with the whisk attachment or whisking vigorously by hand, whip until stiff peaks form (see page 106).

5. Using an electric mixer or creaming vigorously with a wooden spoon, beat the butter and sugar together in a large bowl until light and fluffy. Beat in the egg yolks, then the honey, vanilla, and buttermilk. Add the flour mixture and stir to combine, then gently fold in the egg whites. Gently spoon the batter into the pan atop the pecan halves.

6. Bake for 35 to 40 minutes, until a toothpick inserted into the center comes out clean.

7. Let cool for a few minutes, then flip onto a serving platter. You may think that your cake pan and baking sheet are completely destroyed by burnt honey. They aren't. Just soak them a bit and they'll clean right up! Trust us.

Spiced Parsnip Cake

MAKES ONE 9 BY 13-INCH (23 BY 33CM) CAKE; SERVES 15 TO 20

Cake

2 cups (250g) all-purpose flour

½ cup (55g) almond flour (see tip below)

½ cup (40g) unsweetened shredded dried coconut

2½ teaspoons baking powder

1 teaspoon baking soda

⅛ teaspoon salt

1 teaspoon quatre épices

½ teaspoon ground cinnamon

¼ teaspoon ground ginger

¾ cup (170g) superfine sugar

½ cup (110g) unsalted butter, melted and cooled

½ cup (120ml) buttermilk, at room temperature

½ cup (120ml) maple syrup, preferably Grade B

4 eggs, at room temperature

1 teaspoon vanilla extract

2 cups (150g) shredded parsnips (about 2 large parsnips)

Glaze

¼ cup (60ml) maple syrup, preferably Grade B

¼ cup (60g) unsalted butter

½ cup (120ml) buttermilk, at room temperature

Parsnips do more than stand in for carrots here; they actually transform this dessert into something lighter, airier, and more delicate than any carrot cake we've ever had. If you have difficulty tracking down quatre épices, don't fret: simply mix together ¼ teaspoon each of ground pepper, ground cloves, ground nutmeg, and ground ginger.

1. Preheat the oven to 325°F (165°C) with a rack near the center. Butter a 9 by 13-inch (23 by 33cm) glass baking pan or mist with nonstick spray.

2. To make the cake, combine the flour, almond flour, coconut, baking powder, baking soda, salt, quatre épices, cinnamon, and ginger in a large bowl and whisk for 30 seconds to aerate the flour and mix the ingredients.

3. In a medium bowl, combine the sugar, butter, buttermilk, maple syrup, eggs, and vanilla and whisk until the sugar is dissolved and the ingredients are well blended. Pour into the flour mixture and stir until just a few small pockets of flour remain. Fold in the parsnips. Pour the batter into the prepared pan and spread it evenly.

4. Bake for 35 to 40 minutes, until the center springs back when pressed lightly or a toothpick inserted into the center come out clean.

5. Meanwhile, make the glaze. Combine the maple syrup and butter in a microwave-safe container and microwave in 30-second intervals until the maple syrup starts to boil and the butter is melted or close to it. Let cool for several minutes, then whisk in the buttermilk.

6. Put the cake, still in its pan, on a wire rack, pierce its surface with a fork (to allow the glaze to better seep in), and immediately pour the glaze over the top, trying not to let much drip between the cake and the sides of the pan. Allow the glaze to cool for several minutes before serving.

How to Make Nut Flour without Making Nut Butter

To guarantee that you end up with a light nut flour, not a dense nut butter, follow these two rules: make sure the food processor bowl and blade are completely dry, and make sure the nuts are at room temperature, not cold from the fridge.

Chocolate Dump-It Cake

MAKES ONE 9-INCH (23CM) TUBE CAKE; SERVES 10

Cake

2 cups (400g) sugar

4 ounces (115g) unsweetened chocolate

½ cup (110g) unsalted butter

1 cup (240ml) water

2 cups (250g) all-purpose flour

2 teaspoons baking soda

1 teaspoon baking powder

1 teaspoon sea salt

1 cup (240ml) milk

1 teaspoon apple cider vinegar

2 eggs

1 teaspoon vanilla extract

Frosting

1½ cups (255g) semisweet chocolate chips

1½ cups (355ml) sour cream, at room temperature

Here's a chocolate cake that won't hit you over the head with its richness; rather, it will show off its slightly sweet, slightly bitter-chocolate flavor in a more subtle way. The frosting, a simple mix of melted chocolate chips and sour cream, is light and tangy and has a beautiful sheen. Amanda's mother kept this cake in the fridge, and Amanda says, "It is sublime even when cold."

1. Position a rack in the center of the oven with another rack beneath it. Put a baking sheet on the lower rack to catch any drips as the cake bakes. Preheat the oven to 375°F (190°C). Butter and flour a 9-inch (23cm) tube pan.

2. To make the cake, combine the sugar, chocolate, butter, and water in a large saucepan over medium heat. Cook, stirring occasionally, until the chocolate and butter are melted. Remove from the heat and let cool slightly.

3. In a medium bowl, sift together the flour, baking soda, baking powder, and salt. In a small bowl, stir together the milk and the vinegar.

4. Once the chocolate has cooled slightly, whisk in the milk mixture, then the eggs. In several additions, and without overmixing, whisk in the flour mixture just until smooth. Add the vanilla and whisk once or twice to blend. Pour the batter into the prepared pan.

5. Bake on the middle rack for 30 to 35 minutes, until a toothpick inserted into the center comes out clean.

6. Let the cake cool in the pan for 10 minutes. Put a circle of waxed paper on top of the cake, then invert the pan and transfer the cake and its waxed paper cover to a wire rack. Let cool completely.

7. Meanwhile, make the frosting. Melt the chocolate chips (see page 109), then let cool to room temperature. It's important that the chocolate and sour cream be at the same temperature, otherwise the frosting will be lumpy or grainy. Add in the sour cream, ¼ cup (60ml) at a time, stirring after each addition.

8. When the cake is cool, spread the frosting evenly over the top and sides. Leave the cake upside down, frosting the bottom of the cake so that you have a flat surface to work with. This cake is best eaten the day it's made, but you can keep it covered in the fridge for up to 2 days.

Tomato Soup Spice Cake with Cream Cheese Frosting

MAKES ONE 8-INCH (20CM) LAYER CAKE; SERVES 10 TO 12

Cake

2 cups (250g) all-purpose flour

1⅓ cups (265g) granulated sugar

4 teaspoons baking powder

1 teaspoon baking soda

1½ teaspoons ground allspice

1 teaspoon ground cinnamon

½ teaspoon ground cloves

1 (10¾-ounce/305g) can condensed tomato soup

½ cup unsalted butter (110g) or shortening (100g), melted

2 eggs

¼ cup (60ml) water

1 cup (145g) raisins

Cream Cheese Frosting

½ cup (110g) unsalted butter, at room temperature

8 ounces (225g) cream cheese, at room temperature

2 to 3 cups (250 to 375g) sifted confectioners' sugar

Additional flavorings such as 1 teaspoon vanilla, ½ teaspoon finely grated lemon zest, or ¼ teaspoon ground cinnamon or allspice (optional)

Don't let the can of Campbell's tomato soup in the ingredient list freak you out. Former editor Marian Bull's late grandmother, Ruthie, dared to go there, and we're glad she did. Despite the inclusion of an unusual ingredient—which apparently originated with Irish immigrants looking for cheap alternatives to bake with—the result is a rich and complex spice cake that wants for a soft cream cheese frosting. Serve it up and ask all of your guests to guess the secret ingredient.

---

1. Preheat the oven to 350°F (175°C). Butter and flour two 8-inch (20cm) round cake pans, then shake out any excess flour.

2. To make the cake, in a large bowl, whisk together the flour, granulated sugar, baking powder, baking soda, allspice, cinnamon, and cloves. Add the soup, butter, eggs, and water and, using an electric mixer or whisking vigorously by hand, beat until smooth (and pink!). Fold in the raisins. Pour into the prepared pans.

3. Bake for 35 to 40 minutes, until a toothpick inserted into the center comes out clean and the cake springs back to the touch. Let the cake cool completely before frosting.

4. Meanwhile, make the frosting. Using a stand mixer fitted with a paddle attachment or a handheld electric mixer, beat the butter and cream cheese together until light and fluffy. Gradually add 2 cups (250g) of the confectioners' sugar, then add the remaining confectioners' sugar as needed to create the desired consistency. Mix in the additional flavoring ingredients to the frosting, if desired.

5. You can either frost just the top of each layer, leaving the sides of the cake unfrosted, or cover the entire cake in frosting, sides included (see page 123 for details on assembling and frosting a cake). To frost just the tops of the layers, use half of the frosting atop each one. To frost both the tops and the sides, put one layer of the cake on a serving plate and spread about one-third of the frosting evenly over the top. Set the other layer on top, bottom (flat) side up, and spread the remaining frosting over the top and sides of the cake.

Special Occasion Cakes

Brown Butter Cupcake Brownies

MAKES 12 TO 14 CUPCAKES

1¼ cups (285g) unsalted
butter

2¼ cups (450g) granulated
sugar

1½ cups (130g) unsweetened
cocoa powder (natural or
Dutch-processed)

1 tablespoon water

2 teaspoons vanilla extract

¾ teaspoon salt

4 cold eggs

⅔ cup (85g) all-purpose
flour

1¾ cups (175g) walnuts,
finely chopped

1 cup (170g) bittersweet or
semisweet chocolate chips,
or as desired

Confectioners' sugar,
for dusting (optional)

It takes a real stroke of genius to improve on something that's already so gosh-darn perfect, but such is the case with these gooey-centered cupcake brownies: Food52 contributor Phyllis Grant adapted them from the brilliant Alice Medrich's Cocoa Brownies with Brown Butter and Walnuts, published in *Sinfully Easy Delicious Desserts*. These have all of the benefits of molten lava cakes (chocolate goo! theatrical awe!) with none of the stress—their liquid centers comes from stuffing chocolate chips into the middle of each cupcake before baking. Once baked, they freeze wonderfully: to reheat, just put the frozen cupcakes in a 325°F (165°C) oven for 15 minutes to awaken the gooey center. For an extra flourish, serve topped with ice cream.

---

1. Preheat the oven to 325°F (165°C). Generously butter and flour a nonstick muffin tin, or line the cups with large cupcake papers.

2. Melt the butter in a large saucepan over medium-low heat, swirling it until it starts to brown and smell nutty, about 8 minutes. Remove from the heat and immediately stir in the granulated sugar, cocoa, water, vanilla, and salt. Let cool for 5 minutes.

3. Add the eggs one at a time, whisking well after each addition. Add the flour and mix vigorously for about 1 minute. Stir in the walnuts.

4. Spoon the batter into the prepared muffin tin, distributing it evenly; it's okay to fill the muffin cups almost to the top edge because these cupcakes barely rise. (You may have one or two extra cupcakes. Either bake them after the first batch has come out of the pan and the pan is again cool, or prepare a couple of cups of a new muffin tin, filling the empty spots with a couple of tablespoons of water each.) Press some of the chocolate chips into the center of each cupcake to create a chocolate center.

5. Bake for about 15 minutes, until the edges are set but the middle is still a bit gooey. If need be, cut into one cupcake with a paring knife to determine whether the batter is set.

6. Let cool in the pan for 10 minutes, then remove each carefully. Serve right away, dusted with confectioners' sugar, if desired. Store leftovers in a resealable bag at room temperature for up to 3 days, or freeze for a few months.

Maple Persimmon Upside-Down Cake with Maple Cream

MAKES ONE 10-INCH (25CM) CAKE; SERVES 8 TO 10

Cake

8 tablespoons (110g) unsalted butter

1 cup plus 2 tablespoons (265ml) maple syrup, preferably Grade B

1 egg, at room temperature

1 egg yolk, at room temperature

1½ cups (190g) all-purpose flour

1 teaspoon baking powder

½ teaspoon baking soda

½ teaspoon salt

½ teaspoon ground cinnamon

¼ teaspoon ground nutmeg

⅔ cup (160ml) buttermilk

½ cup (60g) toasted pecans, finely chopped

2 or 3 ripe Fuyu persimmons, sliced crosswise about ¼ inch (6mm) thick

Maple Cream

1 cup (240ml) heavy cream, chilled

2 tablespoons maple syrup, chilled

⅛ teaspoon ground cinnamon

This might be our favorite way to show off ripe, bright-orange persimmons (and to make the most of any that are not at their prime). The fruit forms a beautiful layer atop a maple-sweetened spice cake that's perfect for winter weekend fare. Be sure to use Fuyu persimmons; Hachiyas are softer and more likely to break down under the weight of the cake. And don't skip the slightly sweet maple cream topping—you'll want to eat it on everything, or straight from a spoon.

1. Put a rack in the center of the oven and preheat the oven to 350°F (175°C).

2. To make the cake, put 2 tablespoons of the butter and 2 tablespoons of the maple syrup in a 10-inch (25cm) cast-iron skillet and cook over low heat, stirring a time or two, just until the butter melts.

3. Using an electric mixer or creaming vigorously with a wooden spoon, beat the remaining 6 tablespoons (85g) of butter and 1 cup (240ml) of maple syrup until thoroughly combined, about 2 minutes. Scrape down the bowl, add the egg and egg yolk, and beat for another minute.

4. In a medium bowl, whisk together the flour, baking powder, baking soda, salt, cinnamon, and nutmeg. Add half of the mixture to the butter mixture and beat for 10 seconds. Add the buttermilk and beat for 10 seconds more. Add in the remaining flour mixture, beat for 10 seconds, scrape down the bowl, and then beat for 20 seconds longer. Stir in the pecans, scraping down the bowl in the process.

5. Tilt the skillet to evenly coat the bottom and sides of the pan with the butter and maple syrup mixture. Place one slice of persimmon in the center of the pan, then arrange the remaining slices in slightly overlapping concentric circles working out to the edges of the skillet and covering the bottom of the skillet completely.

6. Carefully pour the batter over the persimmons and smooth the surface with a rubber spatula.

CONTINUED

7. Bake on the center rack for 20 minutes, then rotate the pan and bake for 25 to 30 minutes longer, until the cake is slightly browned and a tester inserted into the center comes out clean.

8. Let cool until the pan can be handled safely without oven mitts, anywhere from 20 minutes to 1 hour or more. Run a thin knife or small offset spatula around the edge to gently loosen the cake. Invert a large serving plate on top of the pan. Bracing the plate against the pan with one hand, flip the cake over, out of the pan, and onto the plate. (Because the pan is so heavy, if someone can help with this, all the better.) Let the cake cool completely.

9. Meanwhile, make the maple cream. Put the cream, maple syrup, and cinnamon in a cold, clean bowl. Using an electric mixer fitted with the whisk attachment or whisking vigorously, whip until soft peaks form (see tip below). Refrigerate the maple cream until you serve the cake.

10. Put a big dollop of maple cream on each slice before serving.

How to Whip Cream

Before you begin, make sure your equipment and ingredients are cold. Chill the cream well before starting to whip and freeze the whisk and the metal bowl you'll be using (we recommend a big balloon whisk and a large deep bowl) for at least 15 minutes. By hand, it will take 3 to 5 minutes of vigorous whisking to achieve soft peaks—when the cream is light and fluffy and just starts to hold peaks when you pull the whisk away. If using an electric mixer, mix on low speed until the cream thickens in order to prevent splattering. Then increase the speed to medium-high and keep whipping until soft peaks form. This will take less time than whipping by hand, so begin to check after 1 to 2 minutes. Continue to whip the cream to achieve stiff peaks, which stand up straight, at attention, when the whisk or beater is lifted. If the peak flops over at its top, it's not quite at the stiff peak stage (that's known as a medium peak). Keep in mind that cream will continue to stiffen as you fold it, spread it, or pipe it, so if you're planning on using your cream for those purposes (rather than simply inhaling it), err on the side of less stiff.

Tender Yellow Cake with Bittersweet Chocolate Frosting

MAKES ONE DOUBLE-LAYER 8-INCH CAKE; SERVES 10 TO 12

Yellow Cake

2 sticks (1 cup) unsalted butter, softened

2 cups granulated sugar

1½ teaspoons vanilla

3 eggs, at room temperature

1 egg yolk, at room temperature

3 cups all-purpose flour

2 teaspoons baking powder

1 teaspoon salt

1½ cups milk, at room temperature

Chocolate Frosting

2 sticks (1 cup) unsalted butter, softened

3 cups powdered sugar

1½ cups chopped bittersweet chocolate, melted and cooled slightly (see tip on page 109)

⅔ cup sour cream

1 teaspoon vanilla extract

Pinch of salt

If there's one dessert that will bring to mind the joy of childhood birthday parties, it's this one. With tender, buttery cake; milky chocolate frosting; and—for extra cheer—a sprinkle coat, this cake will remind you of turning eight. Bake it to celebrate your next accomplishment (or your next Wednesday—whichever comes first).

---

1. Preheat the oven to 350°F. Grease and flour two 8-inch cake pans.

2. To make the cake, using a handheld electric mixer or creaming vigorously with a wooden spoon, beat the butter and sugar until light and fluffy, 4 to 5 minutes. Add the vanilla and mix to combine.

3. Add the eggs and yolk one at a time and mix to incorporate, scraping well after each addition. In a medium bowl, whisk the flour, baking powder, and salt to combine.

4. Add one-third of the flour mixture and mix on low speed to incorporate. Add half of the milk and mix to incorporate. Repeat with another one-third of the flour, the remainder of the milk, and finish with the flour. Mix just to combine (don't overmix).

5. Divide the batter evenly between the two prepared cake pans. Bake until a toothpick inserted into the center comes out clean, 35 to 40 minutes.

6. Cool the cakes in the pans for 15 to 20 minutes, then unmold and cool completely on wire racks.

7. While the cake cools, make the frosting. Using a handheld electric mixer or creaming vigorously with a wooden spoon, beat the butter and powdered sugar until light and fluffy, 4 to 5 minutes.

8. Add the cooled melted chocolate and mix to combine. Add the sour cream, vanilla, and salt and mix until the mixture is smooth, light, and glossy.

CONTINUED

9. Put one layer of the cake on a serving plate and spread about one-third of the frosting evenly over the top. Set the other layer on top, bottom (flat) side up, and spread the remaining frosting over the top and sides of the cake. (For details on assembling and frosting a cake, see page 123.)

10. Since the icing will firm up, you can store this cake by wrapping it in plastic wrap (or packing it in a plastic container) and keeping it in the refrigerator for up to 5 days.

How to Melt Chocolate

If you're melting a chunk of chocolate, the first step is to chop or break it into pieces for more even melting. To melt chocolate in the microwave, put it in a microwave-safe bowl, cover the bowl with parchment paper, and microwave in 20-second intervals, checking and stirring after each interval, just until the chocolate melts. To melt chocolate on the stove top, use a double boiler, or create a makeshift one using a small saucepan and a heatproof bowl that will span the saucepan. Put a small amount of water in the saucepan (not so much that it touches the bottom of the bowl), bring it to a gentle simmer, put the chocolate in the bowl, and set it atop the saucepan. Stir with a dry spoon until the chocolate is melted and smooth.

How to Easily Separate Eggs

There are two ways to separate an egg without any equipment. The first, more hands-on approach is to crack the egg and run it through your fingers, catching the yoke as the whites slip through. (Make sure you wash your hands thoroughly before using this method.) The second, neater way is to use the halves of the eggshell as cups. Pass the yolk back and forth between the shells, letting the whites drop away until only the intact yolk remains in the eggshell.

Cherry Almond Crumb Cake

MAKES ONE 9-INCH (23CM) ROUND CAKE; SERVES 8 TO 10

Streusel

¼ cup (25g) sliced almonds

¼ cup (50g) light brown sugar

½ cup plus 2 tablespoons (80g) all-purpose flour

⅛ teaspoon baking soda

Pinch of salt

6 tablespoons (85g) unsalted butter, melted and cooled

Filling

1½ cups (235g) pitted cherries (sour or sweet, fresh or frozen)

1 tablespoon all-purpose flour

1 tablespoon granulated sugar, if needed

Cake

1 cup (125g) all-purpose flour

1 teaspoon baking soda

½ teaspoon salt

¼ teaspoon baking powder

6 tablespoons (85g) unsalted butter, at room temperature

½ cup (100g) granulated sugar

2 eggs

⅔ cup (160ml) sour cream

½ teaspoon almond extract

½ teaspoon finely grated lemon zest

This cake has never met an occasion it couldn't win over. Dense and sweet, fruit-studded and topped with a nutty streusel, this almond crumb cake from Food52 contributor and all-star baker Yossy Arefi has found its place at plenty of breakfasts, has pulled up a chair at many teatimes, and has fit in nicely at dessert, warmed and topped with a buxom scoop of ice cream.

---

1. Preheat the oven to 325°F (165°C). Butter and flour a 9-inch (23cm) round cake pan, preferably a springform pan.

2. To make the streusel, gently stir together the almonds, brown sugar, flour, baking soda, and salt in a medium bowl. Add the butter and mix until evenly combined.

3. To make the filling, toss the cherries with the flour and granulated sugar until evenly coated; you can forgo the sugar if a sample cherry tastes sweet enough.

4. To make the cake, in a small bowl, whisk together the flour, baking soda, salt, and baking powder.

5. Using an electric mixer or creaming vigorously with a wooden spoon, beat the butter and granulated sugar together in a large bowl until very light and fluffy, about 5 minutes. Add the eggs one at a time, mixing for 30 seconds after each addition and scraping down the sides of the bowl occasionally to ensure even mixing.

6. Stir in the sour cream, almond extract, and lemon zest. Gently fold in the flour mixture, just until combined.

7. To assemble and bake the cake, pour half of the batter into the prepared pan, then smooth the top with a spatula. Scatter the filling, including any flour and sugar at the bottom of the bowl, over the batter, then gently distribute the remaining batter over the cherries, spreading it evenly; it's okay if the cherries aren't completely covered. Scatter the streusel over the top.

8. Bake for 30 to 40 minutes, until the cake is golden brown and a toothpick inserted into the center comes out clean. Let the cake cool completely in the pan before unmolding and serving.

Black Sesame Cupcakes with Matcha Buttercream

MAKES 12 CUPCAKES

Cupcakes

6 tablespoons (55g) black sesame seeds, preferably pretoasted

1¼ cups (155g) all-purpose flour

1 tablespoon unsweetened cocoa powder

1 teaspoon baking powder

½ teaspoon kosher salt

½ cup (110g) unsalted butter, at room temperature

¼ cup (60g) tahini

¾ cup (150g) granulated sugar

2 eggs

2 teaspoons vanilla extract

⅔ cup (160ml) milk

Buttercream

1 cup (225g) unsalted butter, at room temperature

1½ cups (185g) confectioners' sugar, plus more if desired

1 teaspoon matcha green tea powder, plus more if desired

½ teaspoon vanilla extract

We were starting to worry that cupcakes were becoming passé, but Molly Yeh has given them new life with the help of black sesame seeds, our new favorite flavor. By distilling the nutty toastiness of black sesame seeds into cupcake form, she's created a treat that, in her words, is "delightfully unique without being too weird or inaccessible." Since it can be hard to tell when black sesame seeds are toasted, buy them pretoasted from an Asian market or gourmet grocer.

---

1. Preheat the oven to 350°F (175°C). Line 12 standard muffin cups with paper liners. If your black sesame seeds are not already toasted, toast them in a small pan on the stove top over low heat. When they begin to smell nutty, remove the pan from the heat and let the seeds cool slightly.

2. Grind the sesame seeds into a fine powder using either a coffee or spice grinder or a mortar and pestle.

3. To make the cupcakes, whisk together the ground sesame seeds, flour, cocoa powder, baking powder, and salt in a medium bowl.

4. Using an electric mixer or creaming vigorously with a wooden spoon, beat the butter, tahini, and granulated sugar until pale and creamy. Add the eggs one at a time, beating well after each addition. Stir in the vanilla. Add the flour mixture and beat on low speed to combine, then beat in the milk. Scoop the batter into the muffin cups, distributing it evenly.

5. Bake for about 18 minutes, until the cupcakes have slightly risen, the tops are a bit golden, and a toothpick inserted into the center comes out clean. Let the cupcakes cool for a few minutes in the pan, then transfer them out of the pan and onto a wire rack to cool completely.

6. Meanwhile, make the buttercream. Using an electric mixer or creaming vigorously with a wooden spoon, beat together the butter, confectioners' sugar, matcha powder, and vanilla. Taste and add more sugar or matcha powder if desired.

7. Once the cupcakes are cool, use an offset spatula to spread the buttercream over the tops.

Olive Oil Ricotta Cake with Plums

MAKES ONE 9-INCH (23CM) ROUND CAKE; SERVES 8 TO 10

1 cup (240ml) full-fat ricotta

⅓ cup (80ml) olive oil

1 cup (200g) granulated sugar

1 tablespoon finely grated lemon zest

2 eggs

1½ cups (190g) all-purpose flour

1½ teaspoons baking powder

½ teaspoon salt

¼ teaspoon baking soda

8 to 10 small plums, halved

1 tablespoon honey or granulated sugar, if needed

Confectioners' sugar, for dusting

If this is the only thing you do with plums all year, you won't be sorry. It's disproportionately good compared to the amount of effort required, with olive oil and ricotta keeping the cake nicely moist. Use perfectly ripe plums that you would eat raw. For a more luxurious presentation, top each serving with a dollop of whipped cream or whipped mascarpone.

1. Preheat the oven to 350°F (175°C). Butter and flour a 9-inch (23cm) round springform pan.

2. In a large bowl, whisk together the ricotta, olive oil, granulated sugar, and lemon zest. Add the eggs one at a time, whisking well after each addition.

3. Sift the flour, baking powder, salt, and baking soda directly over the ricotta mixture. If you don't have a sifter, use a dry whisk to stir together the flour, baking powder, salt, and baking soda in a separate bowl and then add it to the ricotta mixture. Stir gently just until combined (see tip below). Pour the batter into the prepared pan, spreading it evenly.

4. If the plums are very tart, toss them with the honey until evenly coated. Arrange them on top of the cake, cut side down.

5. Bake for 55 to 65 minutes, until the top is golden brown, the edges pull away from the pan, and a toothpick inserted into the center comes out clean.

6. Let cool in the pan for 10 to 15 minutes, then remove the cake from the pan and place it on a wire rack to cool a bit longer. Dust with confectioners' sugar and serve slightly warm or at room temperature.

How to Avoid Overmixing

When a recipe warns against overmixing, stop as soon as the dry ingredients are no longer visible. Overmixing can deflate batter and cause excessive gluten development, resulting in tough or dense baked goods. Avoid this by folding rather than stirring. Use a spatula to slice down the middle of the batter and scoop up from one side of the bowl. Give the bowl a quarter turn and repeat until the dry ingredients are just incorporated.

Skillet Spice Cake with Gooey Caramel Bottom

MAKES ONE 10-INCH (25CM) ROUND CAKE; SERVES 8

Caramel
¼ cup (50g) dark brown sugar

2 tablespoons unsalted butter

2 tablespoons molasses

Cake
¼ cup (35g) pine nuts

1⅓ cups (165g) all-purpose flour

1 teaspoon baking powder

½ teaspoon kosher salt

¼ teaspoon baking soda

2 teaspoons ground ginger

½ teaspoon coarsely ground black pepper

½ teaspoon ground cinnamon

¼ teaspoon ground allspice

¼ teaspoon ground cloves

¾ cup (150g) dark brown sugar

6 tablespoons (85g) unsalted butter

⅔ cup (160ml) molasses

⅔ cup (160ml) whole milk

½ teaspoon vanilla extract

Topping
1 cup (240ml) cold heavy cream

½ cup (120ml) cold sour cream

This pudding-like cake is a close cousin to sticky toffee pudding but with a few modern details, like the addition of pine nuts and a tangy whipped topping. Serve this cake warm, right out of the cast-iron skillet you make it in (read: easy cleanup). As the cake cools, the gooey bottom layer will start to harden—just pop it back into the oven for a few minutes to loosen it up.

1. Preheat the oven to 350°F (175°C).

2. To make the caramel, put the brown sugar, butter, and molasses in a 10-inch (25cm) cast-iron skillet. Put the skillet in the oven for about 5 minutes, until the butter melts. Stir the mixture until well combined.

3. To make the cake, spread the pine nuts on a rimmed baking sheet and toast them in the oven until golden brown, 5 to 7 minutes, keeping a close eye on them to prevent burning.

4. Meanwhile, in a large bowl, whisk together the flour, baking powder, salt, baking soda, ginger, pepper, cinnamon, allspice, and cloves.

5. Combine the brown sugar, butter, and molasses in a small saucepan over medium heat and cook, stirring frequently, until the butter melts. Stir in the milk and vanilla. Add to the flour mixture and stir just until combined. Carefully pour the batter over the caramel mixture in the skillet, gently spreading it in an even layer. Sprinkle the toasted pine nuts over the batter.

6. Bake for 25 to 30 minutes, until the top is firm and a toothpick inserted into the center of the cake comes out nearly clean. Let cool in the skillet for a few minutes.

7. To prepare the topping, put the cream and sour cream in a cold, clean bowl. Using an electric mixer fitted with the whisk attachment or whisking vigorously, whip until soft peaks form (see page 106).

8. Cut the cake into wedges and serve warm, passing the whipped cream at the table.

Gluten-Free Lemon Blackberry Corn Cake

MAKES ONE 9-INCH (23CM) ROUND CAKE; SERVES 8 TO 10

3 eggs, separated

½ teaspoon kosher salt

1 cup (200g) granulated sugar

1½ cups (190g) fine-ground cornmeal

¼ cup (30g) tapioca flour

2 teaspoons baking powder

½ cup (110g) unsalted butter

Zest of 1 large lemon, finely grated

2 teaspoons freshly squeezed lemon juice

1 cup (240ml) milk

½ to ¾ cup (70 to 105g) small fresh blackberries

2 tablespoons raw sugar

Serve this cake unadorned for breakfast, or dress it up with whipped cream and more berries for a showier dessert. Feel free to use whatever seasonal fruit looks good, perhaps adjusting the other flavorings accordingly: peaches pair with vanilla and nutmeg; cranberries are complemented by an autumnal mix of allspice, ginger, cloves, and molasses.

---

1. Preheat the oven to 350°F (175°C). Butter a 9-inch (23cm) round springform pan, line the bottom with parchment paper, and butter the parchment paper. (Wrap the bottom with aluminum foil if the pan leaks.)

2. Put the egg whites and ¼ teaspoon of the salt in a clean, dry bowl. Using an electric mixer fitted with the whisk attachment or whisking vigorously by hand, whip until soft peaks form. Gradually add ½ cup (100g) of the granulated sugar and continue whipping until stiff peaks form (see page 106).

3. In a medium bowl, stir together the cornmeal, tapioca flour, baking powder, and remaining ¼ teaspoon of salt.

4. Using an electric mixer or creaming vigorously with a wooden spoon, beat the butter and the remaining ½ cup (100g) of granulated sugar until light and fluffy. Add the egg yolks and continue to beat until light and lemon colored, about 2 minutes. Stir in the lemon zest and juice. Add the cornmeal mixture and milk in several alternating additions, blending until thoroughly combined after each addition. Gently fold in the egg whites until completely incorporated, with as few white blobs as possible.

5. Pour half of the batter into the prepared pan, then scatter half of the blackberries evenly over the batter. Top with the remaining batter, then scatter the rest of the blackberries evenly over the top; they will sink into the batter. Sprinkle the raw sugar evenly over the top.

6. Bake for about 60 minutes, until a toothpick inserted into the center comes out clean. Put the pan on a wire rack. Run a knife around the edge of the pan to loosen the cake completely, then remove the outer ring. If you want to transfer the cake to a serving platter, wait until it has cooled completely, then slide a long, thin spatula between the cake and the base to loosen it from the pan. Transfer using a large spatula.

Banana Cake with Penuche Frosting

MAKES ONE 8-INCH (20CM) LAYER CAKE; SERVES 10 TO 12

Cake

½ cup (110g) unsalted butter, at room temperature

1½ cups (300g) granulated sugar

2 eggs, separated

2 bananas, mashed

½ cup (120ml) buttermilk

1⅔ cups (210g) pastry flour

1 teaspoon baking soda

½ teaspoon salt

¼ teaspoon baking powder

½ cup (about 60g) nuts (optional), chopped

Frosting

½ cup (110g) unsalted butter

1 cup (200g) brown sugar

¼ cup (60ml) milk

1¾ to 2 cups (220 to 250g) confectioners' sugar

This simple-seeming cake, a family recipe from editor Lindsay-Jean Hard, is like your favorite banana bread, but lighter and fluffier, with an airy crumb. The real star here, however, is the frosting: its caramelly, brown sugar milkiness is a perfect complement to the banana.

This recipe is also versatile. You can include the nuts or not, and it's fine to substitute all-purpose flour for the pastry flour. Even if you forget to separate the eggs, no worries; the cake will just have a slightly denser crumb.

1. Preheat the oven to 350°F (175°C). Butter and flour two 8-inch (20cm) round cake pans.

2. To make the cake, using an electric mixer or creaming vigorously with a wooden spoon, beat the butter and granulated sugar until pale and fluffy, 3 to 5 minutes. Add the egg yolks one at a time, mixing until incorporated after each addition and occasionally scraping down the sides of the bowl. Stir in the bananas, then stir in the milk until well combined.

3. In a medium bowl, whisk together the flour, baking soda, salt, and baking powder. Add to the butter mixture, along with the nuts, and stir gently just until combined.

4. Put the egg whites in a clean, dry bowl. Using an electric mixer fitted with the whisk attachment or whisking vigorously by hand, whip until soft peaks form (see page 106). Gently fold the egg whites into the batter. Divide the batter evenly between the prepared pans.

5. Bake for 25 to 30 minutes, until a toothpick inserted into the center of the cake comes out with only dry crumbs rather than wet batter.

6. When the cakes are completely cool and you're ready to assemble it, make the frosting. Melt the butter in a large saucepan over low heat. Stir in the brown sugar and cook, stirring constantly, for 2 minutes. Stir in the milk, increase the heat to medium-high, and cook, stirring constantly, until the mixture comes to a boil. Remove from the heat and let cool until lukewarm. Gradually stir in 1¾ cups confectioners' sugar, then mix vigorously until completely smooth (add the additional ¼ cup of confectioners' sugar if the frosting is too loose. Use the frosting immediately, as it will begin to thicken and stiffen as it sits.

7. Put one layer of the cake on a serving plate and spread about one-third of the frosting evenly over the top. Set the other layer on top, bottom (flat) side up, and spread the remaining frosting over the top and sides of the cake. (For details on assembling and frosting a cake, see page 123.)

8. Since the icing will firm up, you can store this cake by wrapping it in plastic wrap (or packing it in a plastic container) and keeping it in the refrigerator for up to 5 days.

How to Assemble and Frost a Cake

Before you get started, make sure you're working in a cool environment, as frosting can become temperamental when it's too warm. You also want the cake layers to be completely cool. If you store them in the fridge overnight (which will make frosting them significantly easier), wrap them well in plastic wrap.

Another key to a beautiful cake is straight lines. You want the layers to have an even height all the way across; cooling the layers by placing the rounded (top) side down on wire racks can help with this. Use a serrated knife to gently cut off any uneven mounds of cake that formed on the top during baking. Rather than use a sawing motion, it's better to keep the knife in place while rotating the cake on a plate or a cakestand, gently sliding the knife farther into the cake as it rotates. Brush off any excess crumbs with a pastry brush.

If you're frosting the cake directly on the serving platter, put down a generous dab of frosting to prevent the cake from moving around while you frost it. Skip this step if you're frosting on a turntable and you plan to transfer the cake to a platter later. Put the bottom layer on top of the frosting, then slip strips of parchment paper under the bottom of the cake; you'll remove them later and—voilà!—the surface will be clean. Spread a generous amount of frosting evenly over the top of the first layer. Set the second layer on top with its smooth bottom side facing up. Press gently to ensure that the cake is straight and the top layer is secure.

Spread a thin layer of the frosting over the top and sides of the cake to form a crumb layer, a thin coat of frosting that will seal in any crumbs and make the finished product look cleaner. After applying the crumb layer, put the cake in the freezer for 15 minutes. Then apply the rest of the frosting, preferably with an offset spatula. Use the back of a spoon to make decorative swirls, or decorate with sprinkles to your liking.

Pumpkin Pie Crumble

MAKES ONE 9-INCH CAKE; SERVES 12

Crust

¾ cup plus 2 tablespoons (110g) cake flour

½ cup plus 2 tablespoons (125g) granulated sugar

1½ teaspoons baking powder

½ teaspoon kosher salt

½ cup (110g) cold unsalted butter, cut into small pieces

1 egg

Topping

¼ cup (30g) all-purpose flour

¼ cup (50g) granulated sugar

2 tablespoons brown sugar

¼ teaspoon ground cinnamon

2 tablespoons unsalted butter

½ cup (60g) pecans, chopped

Filling

1 (15-ounce/425g) can pumpkin puree

2 tablespoons brown sugar

¼ teaspoon kosher salt

¼ teaspoon ground cinnamon

¼ teaspoon ground allspice

⅛ teaspoon ground cloves

⅛ teaspoon ground ginger

⅛ teaspoon ground nutmeg

1 egg

⅓ cup (80ml) milk

What to bake for dessert is the hardest, cruelest decision to make on Thanksgiving. Usually, we grit our teeth and make room for everything, but with this single dessert—and its shortbread bottom, pumpkin pie layer, and buttery pecan topping—you get your cake, tart, and crumble all in one marvelous creation.

---

1. Preheat the oven to 350°F (175°C). Butter a 9-inch (23cm) round pan with a removable bottom, then line the bottom with parchment paper.

2. To make the crust, stir together the cake flour, granulated sugar, baking powder, and salt in a medium bowl. Add the butter and cut it in until it's the size of peas. Add the egg and stir until the dough starts to come together.

3. Dump the mixture into the prepared pan, then press it evenly into the pan. Bake for about 20 minutes, until it puffs up, then settles down and browns a bit. Remove from the oven but leave the oven on.

4. Meanwhile, make the topping. In a large bowl, stir together the all-purpose flour, granulated sugar, brown sugar, and cinnamon. Cut in the butter and add the pecans, then stir until the mixture starts to come together in clumps.

5. To make the filling, put the pumpkin, brown sugar, salt, cinnamon, allspice, cloves, ginger, and nutmeg in a medium bowl and stir with a whisk or spatula. Mix in the egg. Add the milk and stir until smooth.

6. Pour the filling evenly over the cooled crust, then sprinkle the crumble evenly over the top.

7. Bake for about 40 minutes, until the filling is set and the topping is golden. Let cool completely before removing from the pan.

How to Make Cake Flour at Home

Cake flour has lower protein content (7 to 8.5%) than all-purpose (11%) and is used to make lighter, softer cakes with a fine crumb (think angel food cake). You can replicate cake flour using all-purpose flour and cornstarch. For every 1 cup (125g) of cake flour called for, measure out ¾ cup plus 2 tablespoons (110g) of all-purpose flour. Add 2 tablespoons of cornstarch and whisk to combine, then sift.

Savory Baked Goods

Heavenly Molasses Oatmeal Rolls

MAKES 12 ROLLS

¼ cup (60ml) lukewarm water

2 teaspoons active dry yeast

Pinch of granulated sugar

½ cup (110g) cold unsalted butter, cut into small pieces

¾ cup (175ml) milk

1 tablespoon dark brown sugar

¾ cup (70g) rolled oats, plus more for sprinkling

2 tablespoons molasses

2 teaspoons salt

1 egg, lightly beaten

2½ to 3 cups (315 to 375g) all-purpose flour or bread flour

2 to 3 tablespoons melted butter, for brushing the tops of the rolls

This is one of the most beloved recipes on our site, and for good reason. These rolls are supple and rich, with just a hint of sweetness. If you're a novice bread baker, don't worry: the dough is a cinch to handle (only minimal kneading), and the first rise can be done in the refrigerator, even overnight. Don't skip buttering the rolls when they come out of the oven: there's no smell more heavenly than freshly baked rolls slathered in butter.

———————————————

1. Combine the water, yeast, and granulated sugar in a small bowl and stir until the yeast is dissolved. Let stand for a few minutes, until bubbly. (If it doesn't get bubbly, throw it out and get some new yeast.)

2. Put the butter in a large bowl. Heat the milk in a small saucepan, stirring frequently, until steamy and bubbling but not boiling. Add it to the butter and stir until the butter is melted. Add the brown sugar, rolled oats, molasses, and salt and stir until combined. Let cool until lukewarm.

3. Add the egg to the butter mixture and stir well. Stir in the yeast mixture, then stir in 2½ cups (315g) of the flour. Stir in the remaining flour as needed, a tablespoon or two at a time, until the dough loses its sheen. Let the dough rest for 10 minutes.

4. Scrape the dough into an oiled bowl and turn to coat. Cover with plastic wrap and refrigerate for at least 2 hours and up to 12 hours.

5. Generously butter a 9-inch (23cm) round baking pan. Turn the dough out onto a floured work surface and knead lightly. Cut the dough into 12 pieces. Press each ball into a flat rectangle with your fingers, then roll it up in a small ball and tuck the ends under. Place the rolls seam side down in the prepared pan. Brush with half of the melted butter, then sprinkle with rolled oats, pressing the oats down gently just so that they stick into the dough. Let rise in a warm place for about 2 hours, until doubled in size.

6. Preheat the oven to 350°F (175°C). Bake for 35 to 40 minutes, until the rolls are nicely browned and sound hollow when tapped. The internal temperature should be 190°F (90°C).

7. Transfer the pan to a wire rack and brush generously with the remaining melted butter. Let cool for 5 to 10 minutes before serving.

Black Pepper Popovers with Chives and Parmesan

MAKES 12 POPOVERS

2 cups (475ml) milk

4 eggs

¼ cup (60g) unsalted butter, melted

2¼ cups (285g) all-purpose flour

¼ cup (25g) shredded Parmesan cheese

2 tablespoons chopped fresh chives

1 teaspoon finely grated lemon zest

½ teaspoon fine sea salt

½ teaspoon freshly ground black pepper

Popovers—those little hot air balloons of chewy, airy dough—are so whimsical that you can't *not* love them. Mix some basic ingredients (milk, eggs, butter, flour, and salt) in a bowl, spoon the batter into a muffin tin, and watch your soon-to-be pastries puff in the oven. These popovers rise above and beyond the plain variety because they're flecked with flavor from black pepper, Parmesan cheese, chives, and lemon zest. If you do want a simpler popover, leave those ingredients out. Or, for a sweet version, substitute sugar and spices for the savory ingredients and dust the popovers with confectioners' sugar when they emerge from the oven.

1. Preheat the oven to 450°F (230°C). Lightly coat a 12-cup popover pan or muffin tin with melted butter or oil. Put the pan in the oven to heat for 7 minutes.

2. In a large bowl, whisk together the milk, eggs, and butter until well blended. Add the flour, Parmesan, chives, lemon zest, salt, and pepper and mix well. Transfer the batter to a 4-cup (1L) liquid measuring cup. Pour it into the popover pan, dividing it evenly among the cups.

3. Bake for 18 to 20 minutes, then turn the oven down to 350°F (175°C). Bake for 12 to 18 minutes longer, until the popovers are deep golden brown.

4. Let cool briefly in the pan before removing and serving. To reheat cooled popovers, put them in a 350°F (175°C) oven for about 5 minutes.

Fifteen-Minute Olive Oil and Sesame Seed Crackers

MAKES 20 FIST-SIZE CRACKERS (OR BREAK THEM INTO WHATEVER SIZE YOU'D LIKE)

3 ½ cups (440g) all-purpose flour

1 ½ teaspoons salt

1 teaspoon baking powder

1 cup (240ml) water

⅔ cup (160ml) olive oil

Toppings: salt, sesame seeds, herbs, or a combination

Yes, those fancy artisan crackers on grocery store shelves are delicious, but what the packaging doesn't tell you is that they're just as easy to make at home as they are to buy. In the time it would take you to go to the store and pick up a package, you can have wholesome, nutty crackers fresh from the oven. You—or a strong friend—will need to exert some arm power to roll the dough until it's super thin (cracker-thin, you might say), but the results are worth it: crispy crackers to top with dips and cheeses at your next dinner party—or to eat as a snack to get you through the afternoon.

1. Preheat the oven to 400°F (200°C).

2. In a large bowl, stir together the flour, salt, and baking powder. Add the water and olive oil and stir until the dough comes together.

3. Transfer to a 14 by 17-inch (35 by 43cm) rimless baking sheet and knead a few times, then roll out the dough until it is very thin, aiming for ¼ inch (6mm) or thinner. Sprinkle evenly with the toppings of your choice, then gently roll with the rolling pin to press the toppings into the dough.

4. Bake for 6 to 8 minutes, depending on thickness, until the edges begin to turn brown. The crackers will crisp as they cool, so keep a close eye on them and take them out just as they begin to brown.

5. Let cool completely before breaking into pieces. If the cooled crackers aren't as crisp as you'd like them, return them to a warm oven for a few minutes to crisp up.

Cheese Crispettes

MAKES ABOUT 70

1 cup (125g) all-purpose flour, sifted

½ cup (110g) unsalted butter, at room temperature

1 cup (115g) grated sharp Cheddar cheese

¼ teaspoon kosher salt, plus more for sprinkling

½ teaspoon smoked paprika, plus more for sprinkling

¼ to ½ teaspoon cayenne pepper

1 cup (about 80g) panko breadcrumbs

This recipe harks back to the 1960s, when Barbara Reiss (known on Food52 as drbabs) watched her mother make them with margarine and Rice Krispies. In the new millennium, they're made with butter and crispy panko breadcrumbs but deliver similar results: cheesy, flaky, and slightly spicy appetizers that your guests will fill up on before dinner is served. You can make the dough the morning or afternoon of a party, then bake the crispettes as guests start to arrive to entice them with the smell of baking cheese. If you want to make the crispettes gluten-free, Barbara recommends replacing the all-purpose flour with chickpea flour and the panko crumbs with the ever-reliable Rice Krispies.

1. Preheat the oven to 350°F (175°C). Line two baking sheets with parchment paper.

2. Put the flour, butter, cheese, salt, paprika, and cayenne in a food processor and pulse until the ingredients are completely blended and come together to form a ball. Taste and adjust the seasonings as desired.

3. Add the panko and pulse as few times as possible to incorporate them into the dough.

4. Scoop out small amounts of dough, about ½ teaspoon per crispette, and roll them into balls. Place them on the lined baking sheets, spacing them about 2 inches (5cm) apart, then flatten with a fork or spatula. Alternatively, roll the dough out to a thickness of about ½ inch (1.3cm) and use small cookie cutters. Sprinkle the tops with smoked paprika and salt if desired.

5. Bake for about 15 minutes, until lightly browned on the bottom and cooked through. The crispettes are more flavorful on the well-done side, so you may want to bake them a little longer; just watch carefully so they don't burn.

6. Transfer to a wire rack and let cool completely before serving.

Basil Onion Cornbread

MAKES ONE 8-INCH (20CM) SQUARE CORNBREAD; SERVES 6 TO 8

1 teaspoon vegetable oil

1 small sweet onion, finely chopped

1 teaspoon kosher salt, plus a pinch

¼ cup (60g) unsalted butter

1 cup (125g) all-purpose flour

1 cup (160g) cornmeal

1 tablespoon packed light brown sugar

1½ teaspoons baking powder

¼ teaspoon baking soda

1 cup (240ml) plain Greek yogurt

1 egg

½ cup (120ml) whole milk

About ¾ cup (40g) fresh, raw corn kernels (from 1 to 2 ears of corn)

1 tablespoon finely chopped fresh basil

This cornbread breaks from tradition by incorporating Greek yogurt, sautéed onions, and fresh basil. And now that we've made it with these updates, we're not sure we're going back. It deserves a place alongside any stew or chili, and it's also wonderful by itself, warm from the oven, with a thick blanket of butter.

---

1. Preheat the oven to 400°F (200°C). Butter an 8-inch (20cm) square baking pan.

2. Heat the oil in a small skillet over medium heat. Add the onion and a pinch of salt and sauté until the onion is soft and deep golden brown. Let cool slightly.

3. Melt the butter and let it cool slightly.

4. In a medium bowl, whisk together the flour, cornmeal, brown sugar, baking powder, baking soda, and salt.

5. In a small bowl, whisk together the yogurt, egg, milk, onion, and melted butter. Gently stir into the flour mixture just until combined; don't overmix. Stir in the corn and basil. Pour the batter into the prepared pan and smooth the top.

6. Bake for 25 to 30 minutes, until a toothpick inserted into the center comes out clean. Let cool before slicing and serving.

Savory Galette with Greens and Gruyère

MAKES ONE 10-INCH (25CM) GALETTE; SERVES 6 TO 8, FEWER IF SERVING AS A MAIN

Crust

½ cup (110g) salted butter

½ cup (60g) whole wheat flour

¾ cup (95g) all-purpose flour

½ teaspoon salt

2 to 3 tablespoons ice water

1 tablespoon apple cider vinegar

Filling

2 tablespoons olive oil

2 large or 3 medium shallots, halved and thinly sliced

3 cloves garlic, minced

Salt

1 bunch lacinato (or other) kale, deveined and torn into bite-size pieces

1 large bunch mustard greens, deveined and torn into bite-size pieces

Black pepper

1 heaping cup (115g) shredded Gruyère cheese

1 heaping tablespoon Dijon mustard

1 tablespoon heavy cream

Shredded Parmesan cheese, for sprinkling

Black pepper

We have already extolled the value of the Summer Fruit Galette (page 61) over a traditional pie, so it shouldn't take much more persuading to convince you to make a savory galette, either: they are pies you eat *for dinner*. They are also one of the most reliable vegetarian entrées you can pull from your repertoire any time a grain salad feels a little too virtuous or pasta a little unimaginative.

If you're keeping pie dough in your freezer (conveniently, it's the same kind you'd use to make a fruit galette), you're halfway there. And once you have a handle on how to make pie crust, you can make a savory galette with whatever vegetables call out to you at the market and whatever kind of cheese is lingering in your refrigerator. Swaddle them in crust and bake until you have something deep golden brown and bubbling and ready to steal whatever show you have planned.

---

1. To make the crust, cut the butter into ½-inch (1.3cm) pieces, put it on a plate, and freeze for 5 to 10 minutes, until firm but not overly hard.

2. In a medium bowl, stir together the flours and salt with a fork or whisk. Add half of the butter to the flour mixture and toss to coat; ideally, you want a flour barrier between your hands and the butter at all times. Cut in the butter with a pastry cutter or by hand, using a snapping motion with your fingers, until the mixture is crumbly. Add the remaining butter, toss to coat, and cut in again, this time pressing the butter into flat sheets, which will make the crust flakier. Stop when all of the butter is either in small pieces the size of peas or lima beans or in small, flat sheets.

3. Combine 2 tablespoons of the ice water with the vinegar, then sprinkle over the flour mixture a tablespoonful at a time, tossing lightly to distribute the liquid evenly through the flour. Stop when the ingredients just come together and a bit of dough holds together when you squeeze it. If it's crumbly, add a bit more water, just a few drops at a time, until the dough holds together when squeezed.

CONTINUED

4. Form the dough into a ball, then pat it into a fat disk. Wrap tightly in plastic wrap and refrigerate for 3 to 12 hours (or freeze for up to 3 weeks and thaw it overnight in the refrigerator before rolling out).

5. To prepare the filling, shortly before you plan to bake the galette, heat the olive oil in a large skillet over medium heat. Add the shallots and sauté until they soften and begin to turn translucent, 5 to 7 minutes. Add the garlic and a generous pinch of salt and sauté until the garlic is fragrant but hasn't begun to brown, 1 to 2 minutes. Add the greens, then toss and stir until the shallots are evenly distributed. Cook, stirring occasionally, until the greens are tender, about 10 minutes. Stir in another pinch of salt and pepper to taste, bearing in mind that the cheese will add a bit of saltiness too. Let cool for about 10 minutes.

6. Transfer the contents of the skillet to a sieve and press to expel as much liquid as you can. Transfer to a bowl or back into the skillet and stir in the Gruyère. Preheat the oven to 400°F (205°F).

7. To assemble and bake the galette, put the dough on a floured work surface and flour the top of the dough and a rolling pin. Roll out the dough to form a rough circle approximately 10 inches (25cm) in diameter and between ¼ (6mm) and ⅛ inch (3mm) thick. Keep rotating the dough as you roll it out so it doesn't stick to the work surface, and sprinkle the dough or work surface with flour as needed to prevent sticking.

8. Line a baking sheet with parchment paper, then transfer the dough to the lined baking sheet by curling it over the rolling pin and then unfurling it. If it's soft, pop it in the fridge for a few minutes to firm up.

9. Spread the mustard evenly over the dough, leaving a 2- to 3-inch (5 to 7.5cm) border. Spoon the greens evenly over the mustard, then fold the dough over the filling. How much of the dough you fold over the filling, making the galette as open or closed as you'd like, is up to you.

10. Brush the cream over the crust, then sprinkle Parmesan cheese evenly over the crust and filling. Top with a few grindings of black pepper.

11. Bake for 35 to 40 minutes, rotating the pan halfway through, until the crust is deep golden brown. Because the filling doesn't need to set, you can slice and serve the galette as soon as it emerges from the oven.

No-Knead Thin-Crust Pizzas

MAKES 3 GOOD-SIZE INDIVIDUAL PIZZAS

2 1/2 cups (315g) all-purpose flour

1/3 cup (50g) semolina flour, plus more for rolling

2 tablespoons whole wheat flour

2 tablespoons rye flour

1 1/2 teaspoons sea salt

1 teaspoon instant yeast

1 cup plus 3 tablespoons (280g) filtered water

Olive oil, for stretching and proofing

Toppings, such as sun-dried tomatoes, roasted garlic, and mozzarella cheese

To knead or not to knead? To us, that isn't even a question. When we don't need to knead, we just don't do it. We're not going to pretend that it's easier to make this pizza dough than to order pizza for delivery, but this no-knead crust recipe is fairly simple. Once you've experienced the thrill of making your own pizza, you'll probably want to perfect your practice. Heck, you might even decide to invest in a pizza stone. And for the rare occasions when you're not in the mood for pizza, this basic recipe will still come in handy because you can also use it to make great bread sticks (page 144).

If you want to save some of your pizza dough for later, wrap it in plastic wrap after its 8-hour rise and keep it refrigerated for up to two days. Or store it in the freezer and defrost it overnight in the refrigerator. Proceed with the recipe, placing it on the counter 40 minutes before you're ready to bake (step 4).

---

1. In a large bowl, stir together the flours and salt. Add the yeast and water and stir until thoroughly combined. Cover with a clean kitchen towel and let rest for 20 to 30 minutes.

2. Drizzle a teaspoon or so of olive oil around the edges of the dough. Using a large spatula or your hand, lift up half of the dough from the bottom and fold it over the top, making sure the oil lightly coats the surface of the dough. Give the bowl a quarter turn and repeat, then do that six or seven more times.

3. Drizzle another teaspoon or so of olive oil into the bottom of a container that's at least twice the size of the dough and has a tight lid. Put the dough in the container, cover, and refrigerate for at least 8 hours. (If you don't have a large enough container, use a bowl or a pot and cover it tightly with plastic wrap.)

4. Remove the dough from the refrigerator about 40 minutes before you plan to bake. At that time, prepare the oven. Place one shelf in the bottom third of the oven and, if baking more than one pizza at a time, place another shelf in the top third of the oven. If you have a baking stone, put it on the

CONTINUED

lower oven shelf. Preheat the oven to 450°F (230°C) and, if not using a pizza stone, line a baking sheet with parchment paper.

5. Right after you turn on the oven, generously sprinkle semolina flour on your work surface. Cut the dough into three pieces (or four for smaller pizzas). Sprinkle a bit of semolina flour on each and shape it into a ball. Cover with a clean kitchen towel and let rest for 10 to 15 minutes.

6. Sprinkle more semolina flour on the work surface and, keeping the other balls covered, press one ball down with the palm of your hand.

7. Sprinkle a bit more semolina flour on the dough, then use a rolling pin to roll it out evenly in all directions, flipping the dough over and sprinkling a bit more semolina flour on it and the counter as necessary to keep it from sticking; alternatively, stretch and press the dough into a circle or rectangle by hand. For a crisp crust, roll or stretch the dough as thinly as you can. If baking two pizzas at once, you'll roll out another ball of dough and bake one in the top third of the oven and the other in the bottom third.

8. Transfer to the lined baking sheet or, if using a baking stone, transfer to a floured pizza peel or rimless baking sheet lined with parchment. Cover with whatever toppings you desire. Put the baking sheet on the lower oven shelf or, if using a baking stone, transfer the pizza and parchment paper by swiftly jerking the rimless baking sheet.

9. Bake for 6 minutes, then check the pizza and rotate if necessary. Cook for 2 to 6 minutes longer, until the crust is lightly browned all over.

10. Repeat the process for the remaining dough. It's fine to roll out all of the balls before putting on the toppings, but you may find that the first balls will have risen a bit by the time you've shaped the last one. If this is the case, and if you prefer a thinner crust, stretch and press the dough out again before adding the toppings.

CONTINUED

For Something Different

Kale and Ricotta Pizza Tear up 3 or 4 leaves of lacinato kale. Add a drizzle of olive oil, 3 tablespoons of lemon juice, 1 teaspoon of kosher salt, and freshly cracked pepper to taste. Massage the kale until the leaves are dark and soft. Set aside for 20 minutes. When you've rolled the pizza dough and you're ready to start topping, drop 1 cup (240ml) of ricotta cheese in small dollops over the dough. Sprinkle the kale over the top, then garnish with red pepper flakes, sea salt, and another drizzle of olive oil. Bake as instructed.

No-Knead Bread Sticks Prepare and refrigerate the dough as directed. After removing it from the refrigerator (step 4), prepare the oven: Place one shelf in the bottom third of the oven and another shelf in the top third of the oven. Preheat it to 450°F (230°C) and line two baking sheets with parchment paper. Cut the dough in half and shape each piece into a rectangle. Cover with a clean kitchen towel and let rest for at least 15 minutes.

Generously dust the work surface with semolina flour. Keeping one piece of dough covered, roll out the other piece into a rectangle measuring about 7 by 9 inches (18 by 23cm), flipping the dough once or twice and sprinkling with a bit more semolina flour to prevent sticking.

Using a pizza cutter or a metal dough scraper, cut the dough into lengthwise strips, about ¾ inch (2cm) wide. Transfer to one of the lined baking sheets, spacing the strips about 2 inches (5cm) apart; or for fancier bread sticks, twist them as follows: Taking one strip at a time, lift the end that's closest to you and gently bring it together with the other end, gently folding the dough in half and keeping the strip on the work surface. Twist the folded strip while pulling lightly on each end, being careful not to stretch the middle, so that it folds and twists on itself like a simple tassel. Transfer to the lined baking sheet, stretching the bread stick very gently to lengthen it a bit if desired.

Mist lightly with water, then sprinkle on toppings like flaky sea salt, freshly ground pepper, sesame seeds, lightly crushed fennel seeds, finely chopped fresh rosemary, or shredded Parmesan. Let rise for 10 to 15 minutes, preparing the remaining bread sticks in the same way in the meantime.

Bake in the top and bottom thirds of the oven for 6 minutes, then check and rotate if need be. Bake for 2 to 4 minutes longer, until lightly browned all over. Makes approximately 16 bread sticks.

Grilled Flatbreads

MAKES 4 MEDIUM FLATBREADS

3 cups (375g) bread flour

1 teaspoon kosher salt

1 teaspoon instant yeast

1¼ cups (300ml) warm water

¼ cup (60ml) extra-virgin olive oil, plus more for brushing

Flaky sea salt, for sprinkling

Leaves from 1 or 2 sprigs rosemary, for sprinkling

Our test kitchen manager Erin McDowell is a pie wizard and pastry whisperer who seems to churn out dozens of masterpieces in the blink of an eye. We thank her for this recipe for grilled flatbread, which makes it possible to make bread with so little fuss that we wonder why we've been afraid of the process for so long. This recipe will expand your grilling repertoire to include crusty, charred flatbreads that are the ideal canvas for flaky sea salt and fresh herbs. We also love them slathered with pesto and ricotta cheese and topped with fresh vegetables. Eat them as soon as they come off the grill, or use them over the next few days to make beautiful open-faced sandwiches. They make a great vessel for hummus or other dips and can also be packed up for a good picnic lunch. Try them with chicken salad or—our personal favorite—sprinkled with pistachio dukkah (see page 146).

1. In a large bowl, whisk together the flour and salt. Whisk in the yeast. Make a well in the center of the flour and pour in the water and olive oil. Stir with a wooden spoon until the dough comes together in a shaggy mass.

2. To knead by hand, turn the dough out onto a lightly floured work surface and knead until a smooth ball forms, 6 to 9 minutes. If you use a stand mixer fitted with the dough hook, mix for 3 to 4 minutes on medium speed.

3. Oil a medium bowl and transfer the dough to the bowl. Cover loosely and let rise for 30 to 60 minutes, until doubled in size.

4. Preheat a grill or grill pan until smoking hot. Clean and oil the grates of the grill.

5. Meanwhile, divide the dough into four pieces. It will be on the sticky side, so lightly oil your hands to make shaping the dough easier. Grasping the outside edges of a piece of dough, hold it vertically above the work surface and stretch it gently into an oblong, letting gravity do most of the work. Lightly oil both sides of the dough. (One easy way to do this is to put it on an oiled baking sheet. Then, just before placing it on the grill, flip it over to oil the other side.) Shape the remaining pieces the same way.

CONTINUED

6. Grill until golden brown, 3 to 4 minutes per side. When the flatbreads are still hot from the grill, brush with more olive oil and sprinkle with flaky salt and rosemary leaves. Serve warm, or wrap the breads in aluminum foil or plastic wrap and store in the refrigerator for up to 4 days. Reheat gently in a warm oven before serving.

For Something Different

Pistachio Dukkah Toast 3 tablespoons of coriander seeds and 1 tablespoon of cumin seeds in a small skillet over medium heat until fragrant, about 2 minutes. Transfer them to a spice grinder, mortar and pestle, or mini food processor and allow to cool. Meanwhile, toast ½ cup (60g) shelled pistachios in a small skillet until golden, about 5 minutes. Transfer to a cutting board and finely chop. Set aside. Add ¼ cup (40g) sesame seeds to the skillet and toast until golden brown, about 2 minutes, and set aside. Toast 3 tablespoons dried, unsweetened shredded coconut in the skillet, stirring constantly until golden, about 2 minutes. Now grind the spices until you have a fine mixture and add them to a bowl with the coconut, sesame seeds, pistachios, 1 teaspoon of sea salt, and ½ teaspoon of ground pepper.

Baking for Any Occasion

You may be having a hard time choosing between these recipes—we hope that this guide will help make your decision at least a bit easier. Whether you're baking for a casual brunch, a school bake sale, or a celebratory dinner, here are the recipes that will serve you best.

FOR BAKE SALES

Cranberry, Oatmeal, and Flaxseed Muffins | 11

Cream Cheese Cookies | 25

Cardamom Currant Snickerdoodles | 29

Grape-Nut and Chocolate Chip Kitchen Sink Oatmeal Cookies | 30

Six-Ingredient Peanut Butter and Jelly Sandwich Cookies | 33

Hippie Crispy Treats | 41

Black Sesame Cupcakes with Matcha Buttercream | 112

FOR BAKING WITH KIDS

Bestest Banana Bread | 15

Overnight Orange Refrigerator Rolls | 19

Cardamom Currant Snickerdoodles | 29

Six-Ingredient Peanut Butter and Jelly Sandwich Cookies | 33

Hippie Crispy Treats | 41

Blueberry Schlumpf | 51

No-Knead Thin-Crust Pizzas | 141

FOR SOMEONE SPECIAL ON VALENTINE'S DAY

Balsamic Macaroons with Chocolate Chips | 38

Magic Espresso Brownies | 46

Chocolate Dump-It Cake | 96

Brown Butter Cupcake Brownies | 102

Tender Yellow Cake with Bittersweet Chocolate Frosting | 107

FOR COMMITTING TO MEMORY

Cranberry, Oatmeal, and Flaxseed Muffins | 11

Whole Wheat Molasses Yogurt Bread with Figs and Walnuts | 12

Bestest Banana Bread | 15

Cream Cheese Cookies | 25

Double-Layer Coconut Pecan Bars | 42

Blueberry Schlumpf | 51

Apple Brown Betty with Gingersnap Crumbs | 55

FOR YOUR FREEZER

Featherweight Blueberry Scones | 2

Grape-Nut and Chocolate Chip Kitchen Sink Oatmeal Cookies | 30

Dark Chocolate and Cherry Mandelbrot | 34

Brown Sugar Shortbread | 37

Cold-Oven Pound Cake | 91

Brown Butter Cupcake Brownies | 102

FOR WHEN IT'S COLD OUTSIDE

Pudding Chômeur | 75

Baked Rice Pudding with Coconut Milk and Honey | 76

Lemon Sponge Cups | 79

Maple Persimmon Upside-Down Cake with Maple Cream | 105

Skillet Spice Cake with Gooey Caramel Bottom | 116

Acknowledgments

If it takes a village to raise a child, it takes an entire online and in-person community to produce a book.

A huge thank you to James Ransom, whose commitment to producing excellent work is evident on every page of this book. Thank you for your patience and diligence, and for being as fussy about creating beautiful images as we are. You made this book come to life. We hope your next projects—Cooking with Photoshop and That's a Wrap—are wildly successful.

Thank you, also, to the kitchen wizards—Allison Buford, Derek Laughren, Erin McDowell, Lisa Nicklin, Anna Gass, and Jennifer Vogliano—who worked endlessly to frost cakes, cut biscuits, and whip egg whites. Your spatula skills are inspiring, as is your sense of humor and your perseverance in the face of an impossible pavlova (it's too bad it didn't work out).

Thank you to Stephanie Bourgeois and the team of recipe testers for responding to our frantic banana bread-related emails at all hours of the day and working hard to guarantee the recipes are exactly as intended. We hope you all have enough baked goods stored in your freezer to last a lifetime.

Thank you to the entire team at Ten Speed Press: Emily Timberlake, Hannah Rahill, Aaron Wehner, Jasmine Star, and Karen Levy, for your edits and re-edits and for the cross-country packages and conference calls; Ali Slagle, for your brilliant ideas (especially when it came to toppings for French toast); and Emma Campion and Margaux Keres, for your vision.

Thank you to Alexis Anthony for your styling expertise. We are in awe of how effortless you make it look to style linens and compose perfect piles. We admire your work. Thank you to Marian Bull, for your family's funny-named recipes, for your wit and words, and for your styling help. To Kenzi Wilbur and the rest of the Food52 editorial team: thank you for your inspiration and collaboration.

Thank you to Prop Workshop and Good Light Studio. Thank you for letting us call your plates, bowls, and cake stands our own—if only for a week.

Thank you to the entire Food52 community: Your recipes and the stories behind them continue to make us grin. Your creativity in the kitchen is enviable, and your ability to turn ingredients into something delicious, easily, is what this book is all about.

A special thank you to (real names and Food52 usernames): Lindsay-Jean Hard, Alice Medrich, Yossy Arefi, Brette and Sheri Warshaw, Phyllis Grant, Helen Conroy, vvvanessa, FamilyStyle Food, Emily Vikre, Joan Jampel, monkeymom, Liz Larkin, Molly Yeh, ENunn, Barbara Reiss, foxeslovelemons, June Jacobs, TheWimpyVegetarian, Couldn'tBeParve, Emiko Davies, Abbie Argersinger, Posie Harwood, bonbonmarie, Kate Williams, camille, and Sara Grimes. We don't want to know what Food52 would be without you.

Index

Published in the United States by Ten Speed Press, an imprint
of the Crown Publishing Group, a division of Random House
LLC, a Penguin Random House Company, New York.
www.crownpublishing.com
www.tenspeed.com

Ten Speed Press and the Ten Speed Press colophon are
registered trademarks of Random House LLC.

Library of Congress Cataloging-in-Publication Data is
on file with the publisher.

Hardcover ISBN: 978-1-60774-801-4
eBook ISBN: 978-1-60774-802-1

Printed in China

Design by Emma Campion and Margaux Keres

10 9 8 7 6 5 4 3 2 1

First Edition